What they said about the book ...

'Being a middle manager, you're not only respo[...] accountable to those above you – it is a major ju[...] [...]ccounts of her own management journey and the astute advice she has to offer serve as a useful resource for everyone managing in the voluntary sector.'
Mark Davis, Chief Executive, Middlesbrough Voluntary Development Agency

'*It's Murder in Management* is a veritable tour de force and an excellent resource for new and aspiring managers, and even for seasoned managers who need reminding how to deal with the difficulties of their job. Debra provides clarity about roles and responsibilities and gives the reader tools to help work through what is often a huge to-do list. It should be included as part of all new managers' inductions.'
Sarah Hughes, Chief Executive, Centre for Mental Health

'In this book Debra's wise insights are made available to all – you can hear her voice in every sentence and, best of all, she gives really good advice without ever shirking the difficult realities of being a manager. There is so much in here that you can apply to your daily practice with real benefit.'
Jane Ide, Chief Executive, NAVCA

'In *It's Murder in Management*, Debra has pre-digested all the tough lessons of management for you and turned them into essential learning points and sound advice. I might make this book mandatory for all middle managers in my charity!'
Kate Lee, Chief Executive, CLIC Sargent

'Reading this, I became aware of the gentle sound of pennies dropping – and this after over 30 years in the leadership and management of people! Honest and candid, this book reassures leaders of all levels that it is OK to fail; in fact, it is probably compulsory! A great ready-to-use reference: one to dip in and out of to dispel those niggling doubts.'
Alex Lochrane, Chief Executive, Hampshire and Isle of Wight Air Ambulance

'You can't move for people talking about leadership in the charity sector. Leadership and values are what we all like to talk about. Management, on the other hand, is a neglected and underrated art in spite of being vitally important and so difficult to do well. Nurturing good management is essential for charities serious about effecting change and this book is timely in shaking us out of our complacency. It is a valuable resource for charity managers.'
Polly Neate, Chief Executive, Shelter

'I really wish I'd had a copy of this book when I started out! It packs years of experience into a wise, entertaining and insightful guide. None of us are perfect and so Debra helps new managers navigate their new terrain with a surer footing.'
Jacqui Penalver, Transformation Director, Papworth Trust

Debra Allcock Tyler

IT'S MURDER IN MANAGEMENT

The no-fibbing guide for new managers

directory of social change

Published by the Directory of Social Change (Registered Charity no. 800517 in England and Wales)

Head office: Resource for London, 352 Holloway Rd, London N7 6PA

Northern office: Suite 103, 1 Old Hall Street, Liverpool L3 9HG

Tel: 020 7697 4200

Visit www.dsc.org.uk to find out more about our books, subscription funding websites and training events. You can also sign up for e-newsletters so that you're always the first to hear about what's new.

The publisher welcomes suggestions and comments that will help to inform and improve future versions of this and all of our titles. Please give us your feedback by emailing publications@dsc.org.uk.

First published 2018

ISBN 978 1 78482 040 4 (print edition)
ISBN 978 1 78482 041 1 (digital edition)

British Library Cataloguing in Publication Data
A catalogue record for this book is available from the British Library

Illustrations by Grizelda
Cover and text design by Kate Griffith
Typeset by Marlinzo Services, Frome
Printed and bound by Page Bros, Norwich

MIX
Paper from
responsible sources
FSC® C023114

Contents

About the Directory of Social Change

The Directory of Social Change (DSC) has a vision of an independent voluntary sector at the heart of social change. We believe that the activities of independent charities, voluntary organisations and community groups are fundamental to achieve social change. We exist to help these organisations and the people who support them to achieve their goals.

We do this by:

- providing practical tools that organisations and activists need, including online and printed publications, training courses, and conferences on a huge range of topics;
- acting as a 'concerned citizen' in public policy debates, often on behalf of smaller charities, voluntary organisations and community groups;
- leading campaigns and stimulating debate on key policy issues that affect those groups;
- carrying out research and providing information to influence policymakers, as well as offering bespoke research for the voluntary sector.

DSC is the leading provider of information and training for the voluntary sector and publishes an extensive range of guides and handbooks covering subjects such as fundraising, management, communication, finance and law. Our subscription-based websites contain a wealth of information on funding from grant-making charities, companies and government sources. We run more than 300 training courses each year, including bespoke in-house training provided at the client's location. DSC conferences and fairs, which take place throughout the year, also provide training on a wide range of topics and offer a welcome opportunity for networking.

For details of all our activities, and to order publications and book courses, go to www.dsc.org.uk, call 020 7697 4200 or email cs@dsc.org.uk.

About the author

Debra has been the Chief Executive of the Directory of Social Change (DSC) since 2001. She is a Trustee of In Kind Direct, a charity founded by HRH The Prince of Wales, a Trustee of the Berkshire Community Foundation, Vice-President of the Soldiering On Awards, and an Ambassador for women and girls at risk of or affected by female genital mutilation and other harmful practices for the Africa Advocacy Foundation (AAF). She was the founder Chair of the Small Charities Coalition, served as a member of the Charity Commission's SORP Committee for seven years and was the Vice-Chair of Governors of Whiteknights Primary School for some years. Her first volunteering role was at the age of 16, in a local hospice, helping the staff with basic duties such as cleaning and changing beds.

After a brief stint in the private sector, Debra has spent most of her career in the charitable sector. Following a short period as a management consultant in her 20s, she moved into leadership roles covering a range of functions including campaigning, policy development, sales, product development, media relations and training. She is particularly proud of her 14 years as a voluntary Trade Union Officer and the year she spent working with Youth at Risk – an organisation that works with young people suffering severe social disadvantages. She was the first female Programme Director of the Runge Effective Leadership programme and is a mentor and advisor to a number of CEOs and chairs of trustee boards.

Debra is a renowned authority in the field of leadership and governance in civil society and an internationally published author of several books. She writes 'The Last Word' column for *Third Sector* magazine which reaches around 123,000 people per publication. Her interests also include theoretical physics, behavioural economics and politics. Debra has a degree in psychology and is a Fellow of the Royal Society of Arts and a member of the Royal Institution. She admits to being a slave to a basset hound called Arthur.

Acknowledgements

There are so many folk who help you to learn along the way. Below is a list of the ones who have been most involved in my thinking over the last year or so.

But in particular I would like to mention Ian Lawson, who died far too young in early 2018. Ian was a huge part of my leadership journey for over 30 years and I owe much of what I have achieved in my leadership career to his support and wisdom.

Caron Bradshaw
Vicky Browning
William Butler
Stuart Cole
Mark Davis
Bronwen Edwards
Sir Stuart Etherington
Andy Garnett
Grizelda
John Hoare
Emily Hughes
Sarah Hughes
Jane Ide

Catherine Johnstone
Jay Kennedy
Evangeline Kirupairajah
George Knight
Kate Lee
Annette Lewis
Denise Lillya
Alex Lochrane
John Martin
Justin Martin
Alistair Mortimer
Lucy Muir-Smith
Polly Neate

Chi Okpala
Maria Pemberton
Jacqui Penalver
Phyllida Perrett
Satinder Pujji
Lesley Thornley
Jill Thornton
Tom Traynor
Suzanne Tubb
John Wallace
Peter Wanless
Ben Wittenberg
Gabriele Zagnoj

DSC is grateful to the following people and organisations for their permission to reproduce their copyright materials.

Margaret Lloyd for her permission to reproduce material from her and Brian Rothwell's work.

The Work Foundation for their permission to use material from a report by Penny Tamkin, Gemma Pearson, Wendy Hirsh and Susannah Constable, published by the Work Foundation.

Caron Bradshaw for her permission to use her quote from an email to the author.

John Adair for his permission to reproduce his action-centred leadership model – The Three Circles © John Adair.

Foreword

There are a million reasons to read this book if you are either entering into your first management role or have been in the role a little while and are wondering why it is not as straightforward as perhaps you thought it would be.

If I could go back to my first management role and apologise to all those staff on whom I unashamedly practised my leadership style, I would. Of course, I didn't know that what I was doing at the time was learning through practising, and my first two years in the management arena were fraught with a mixture of self-doubt and unbridled exhilaration.

For many of us, the pathway that takes us into management is something we work towards and covet. Friends and families congratulate you on achieving the next stage of your career and, if you are anything like me, you dream about changing the world and making a difference on an expanding stage.

Therefore, it is often quite a shock when the move into management signals the need for you to rethink how you are at work. It sees you entering a completely different space that often is not as you previously perceived it. In this book, Debra focuses on the nuts and bolts of becoming a manager in her usual no-nonsense way. She gets right to the heart of what you need to know, how you need to behave and what will help you nurture your team. There is no hand-wringing or tortured self-examination here but rock-solid and positive advice with a sprinkling of humour.

I encourage you to embrace your management opportunity as the start of a career-long journey of developing your own leadership style and your levels of confidence. Arguably, it is a chance to create a firm platform for your future as a leader. Becoming a manager does not mean you receive instant wisdom and get all the answers overnight, but it does give you the responsibility to nurture, develop and inspire the people who need you to manage them. To achieve the highest levels of success, you will need to invest in developing your inner manager – and reading this book is a great way to start.

Catherine Johnstone CBE
CEO, Royal Voluntary Service

Introduction

If hindsight was foresight, we'd all be geniuses!
Proverb

Why this book? During my career I've operated at all levels in management roles – from team leader all the way up to CEO and chair. Of all of the roles I've been in, I can honestly say that by far and away the hardest and most challenging role is that of a leader at mid-management level. I remember many, many days when I came close to murdering my bosses, my team or my colleagues! I expect you have similar days.

Day in, day out, you will need to find a way to sit alongside your team (either literally or metaphorically) and create a happy, effective working environment which feels warm and friendly while, at the same time, maintaining enough distance that you can effectively deal with poor performance or poor attitudes. This is not easy. It's all very well for those of us now in more senior positions, who probably are able to be a little separate from our teams, to spout on about how you've got to get the balance right – but getting it right? Whole different board game!

But I haven't forgotten how hard it is. And how challenging it can be when you're responsible for implementing decisions that some people may disagree with but where you have to hold the management line, even though you may not have been involved in making those decisions. You have to influence those folk more senior to you, including trustees if you're in a smaller organisation, and yet they're under no real obligation to listen to you. You have to work as part of a wider management team where you may find some of your peers more challenging than others, yet you have to find a way to get on because there's no avoiding it and you can't achieve your team's objectives without others' input. This comes with a whole raft of challenges – but I don't need to tell you that.

I remember when I got promoted to my first management role. I was very young, about 21 or 22 as I recall. I was promoted from within the team I was already in and my teammates were really supportive about my appointment. So I started the job on a wave of enthusiasm – both mine and theirs. It didn't take long for it all to go horribly wrong. I was incredibly inexperienced, hadn't had any training at that stage and was basically winging it. Within three months of being appointed, I had managed to turn a high-performing team of happy people into a low-performing team of seriously pissed-off people! I was being bossy rather than being the manager and it took me a while to understand the difference.

In the end, the team revolted and there was a horribly uncomfortable meeting where they made it very clear what they thought of my management skills! I went home that night in tears. At the time, I was living at home and my father gave me some fantastic advice that I've never forgotten and have used over and over again: tell the truth. He asked me whether there was any truth in their criticism of me. And of course there was – I was a terrible manager! So he suggested that I call the team together the next day and tell the truth: that I could see I wasn't doing a great job but that I really wanted to, and I needed their help to be the best possible manager I could be. That conversation completely revolutionised our relationship and I can now say, hand on heart, that the couple of years that I spent managing that team – when we were all learning together – was one of the happiest working times of my life.

The lesson I learned is to trust people. Most people are on your side and want you to do well – you just have to allow them to help you.

And so I've written this book because I too am on your side. I want you to know you're not alone and there are things that you can do to help make your managerial journey a little bit easier. I want to share with you the practical advice that I so needed when I was learning my management skills, not the relentless theorising that most books present.

I hope that there are things in this book that you will find useful. But, most importantly, remember that you are managing for a great purpose. Remember that, if you do your job well (which you will), you are helping to make society a better place for people. That's got to be worth it.

1 What do managers do?

So much of what we call management consists of making it difficult for people to work.
Attributed to Peter F. Drucker

It can be a bit of a shock – that first time you experience what it feels like to be a manager. When it hits home quite hard that, as a manager, you are not judged on the quality of the work that you personally produce but on the work of your team. When you realise that other people's performance affects yours in a much more personal way than it ever has before.

Here's the thing: everything has now changed. Before it was just you. Others could of course influence your output as a worker, but the actual quality was basically down to you. And you probably did a pretty good job, which helped with you getting promoted. But as a manager your job is fundamentally quite different. It is to get others to deliver. Because you can't do all the work yourself and how well you get others to work is what you will now be judged on. Unfortunately, so often we arrive in our first management or team leader position wholly ill-equipped to deal with the complex and difficult task of getting others to perform.

Many of us get promoted into management positions because we were particularly good at our technical or specialist job. We were the best fundraiser, therapist, accountant, caseworker or some such. However, it's fairly rare that we arrive in our new job with sufficient management training or experience to hit the ground running. Most of us have to learn the hard way and so, if you're reading this book prior to getting your first promotion to a management role, then yay! That gives you a head start. But I strongly suggest you ask for some training in management skills. A basic level of training will help you to avoid some obvious first-level mistakes. In fact, even if you've been in the role for a while, get some training as, I absolutely promise you, it will help.

At the simplest level, there are essentially three core skills of management in most organisations: technical knowledge, administrative abilities and people skills. There are also, generally speaking, four levels of authority. As either a **front-line worker** or a **technical specialist** (for example, a purchase ledger clerk or a fundraiser), what you are hired for is your technical competence. At that stage you are not managing others, although you are probably working within a team. At **team leader level**, you are expected to have a degree of technical speciality, but you also have to know how to manage people and how to administer stuff (i.e. you have to be able to plan, report, budget, etc.). At **middle and senior management level**, your technical competence is less a part of the role. At this level you are largely focused on helping others to deliver on their technical competences and making sure there are plans, projects, monitoring and so on. Finally, at the **CEO level**, you spend the bulk of your time leading people. (For more on what CEOs do, read the sister book to this one: *It's Tough at the Top*.) Of course, in smaller organisations there is a bit more overlap, but you get the gist. The diagram in the next section shows what I mean.

The promotion envelope

The promotion envelope is a commonly used visual representation of how the core parts of your role shift and change as you get promoted and move into more senior management roles.

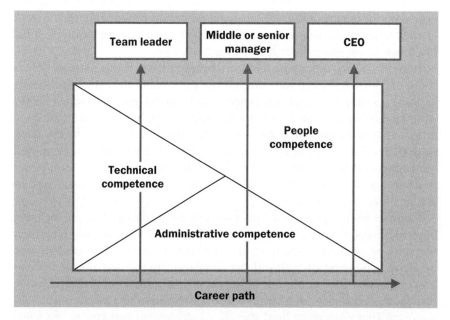

At the early stage of your career, you will probably spend most of your time honing your basic skill base. Some people prefer to stay at the technical or specialist level (for example, specialists in IT, finance or fundraising) and have no desire to move into management. Others, as they get better and better at the job they do, might end up coming to the attention of people in their organisation who are keen to promote them, or they might gain confidence and start applying for management posts in other organisations. Either way, if this is you, you are now in a management position. You have (hopefully!) a higher salary, but you definitely have more responsibility. Your job will have changed fundamentally from being almost solely technical to including a level of general administration of personnel, budgets, reports and so on, as well as leading other people.

The hard part!

The management part of the role, I think, is fairly straightforward. It's a technical skill to be able to budget or write a report and, if you don't know how to do it, these skills can be relatively easily taught or picked up. When it comes to leading people, however, my experience suggests this is probably the most difficult part of the management role, even with training. You become accountable for others' performance and motivation, the quality of their work and, probably the toughest thing to manage, their time-keeping and ability to stick to deadlines.

When your computer plays up, you can ring technical support, who will fiddle with it and make it co-operate. You can switch it off. You can chuck it out and get a new one. But with people? Much as we might quite like to turn them off sometimes – or reboot them to factory settings – we can't. We have to deal with their idiosyncrasies: emotions, fears, passions, strops, bad hair days ...

When you're new to management, or haven't had appropriate training, it's all too easy and tempting to slip back down the envelope into the technical side of the job – which you already know you're good at and where you can hide from having to do the 'people thing'. I've been leading people for over 30 years and there are still days when I'd quite like to go and hide somewhere or when the thought of a job where I don't have to manage anyone is very attractive!

The difference in management levels

In all organisations except the very smallest (say, those of 15 or fewer people), there are generally easily visible levels of management and leadership. This is the case regardless of the type of organisation. There is always a board, for example, but how many hours they work and whether they are paid or not will vary dependent upon the technical construction of the organisation. In practice, however, the responsibilities are largely the same, regardless of the type of organisation and whether the role is paid or unpaid. Most organisations will have:

- board of trustees (with a chair);
- a CEO (or director or secretary general);
- directors and/or senior managers;
- middle management;
- team leaders.

In some smaller organisations, there may not be team leaders per se but rather managers who probably have similar levels of responsibility to middle managers or senior managers in larger organisations. But, either way, you get the point.

What do managers do?

When I was on the front line, I thought I had a pretty good idea of what the level above me did ('not much' was my perception usually!). Then, when I got promoted, I suddenly realised that much of the work my manager did had not been visible to me. It included influencing other levels of management, negotiating resources, managing budgets, communicating with senior management, writing reports and so on, which are generally not noticed by the team. In fact, like many of you, I suspect, I had always thought the level above was better paid for doing a cushier job – how wrong I was! So I think it's helpful to understand that all of the levels above you have specific roles which you may not be aware of.

The board of trustees

In many respects, the role of the board is one of the most critical ones in a charity. The board of trustees of a registered charity are almost always unpaid (although there are a few exceptions). In theory, they are supposed to operate as non-executive directors, which means that they are not actively engaged in running the organisation – their role is oversight. This, however, doesn't always happen in practice and certainly not in smaller charities where there are few, if any, staff. In smaller organisations the board may often end up doing much of the hands-on work of the charity and that is why, for the purposes of governance and accountability, it is important that they understand which hat – trustee's or charity worker's – they are wearing and are able to distinguish when their job is delivery and when it is oversight. Effectively, as board members they are volunteers, which is why you can say in truth that all charities are run by volunteers. Their duty is to ensure that the charity complies with charity law and delivers the charity's objects for the purpose of its beneficiaries. They are held to account for the overall performance of the charity, its work and its money. In smaller organisations, it is possible that trustees will be more involved in the day-to-day running of the organisation but, nonetheless, governance is still a very separate and distinct activity.

Governance effectively means that the trustees are the people with legal and fiscal accountability for what happens in the organisation. They are the ones who, in theory, will be prosecuted and possibly face jail if the organisation is negligent or irresponsible in what it does. That's why sometimes it can feel as if they are a bit of a pain in the derrière. Wouldn't you be if you were accountable for the actions of an organisation where you had little or no control over the day-to-day activities and yet it was your name on the letterhead?

In brief, it is the trustees' duty to ensure that the organisation:

- is complying with the terms of its memorandum and articles of association and with its charitable objects – i.e. those legal documents that specify what the organisation and its trustees are and are not allowed to do;
- is complying with its legal and regulatory obligations, for example regarding health and safety, employment law, financial reporting and charity law;

- has a vision and strategy, which include financial targets and parameters;
- has appropriate mechanisms in place to assess the performance of the CEO.

There is an agreed-upon governance code for charity trustees, which can be found at www.charitygovernancecode.org. It isn't a legal requirement to follow the code, but the code does helpfully outline the key recommendations for and responsibilities of trustees. There are two versions – one for larger charities and one for smaller ones – but, basically, the principles are the same whatever the size of the organisation.

The Charity Governance Code
The following diagram is a useful summary of the seven basic principles of charity governance required of all trustees. It would be possible to add a great deal of detail on what the board is required to do under each heading, but broadly they are accountable for making sure all seven of these things happen and are working effectively within the charity. Although this is specific to charities, in reality the principles apply across most not-for-profit organisations including community interest companies, charitable incorporated organisations and other forms of social enterprise.

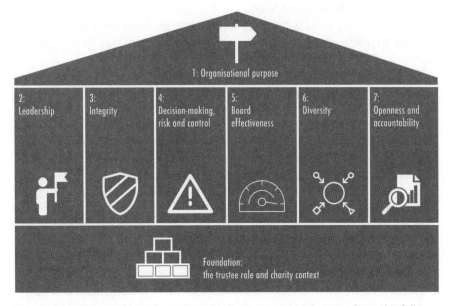

The diagram is reproduced from www.charitygovernancecode.org, where the full code can also be found.

The role of the chair
Contrary to popular myth, there is actually no rule that requires a board of trustees to have a chair or a treasurer unless it is written into the charity's governing documents. Technically, the entire board is accountable for the

performance of the organisation and, unless specified differently in the governing documents, the chair and treasurer do not have additional responsibilities under charity law.

However, most boards will find it sensible to appoint a chair. This is because it is very difficult for the CEO to be managed by the board as a whole, as there are often at least eight people on the board (in some charities the number can go as high as 25!), so a chair is usually appointed for practical reasons. The chair's role is usually to manage the board, provide support to the CEO and monitor the CEO's performance.

The CEO

Under charity law, the CEO is not technically a member of the board. This means that:

- they are not a trustee;
- in the case of a company limited by guarantee, they are not a member or director of the company, which means they have no legal liability;
- they have no voting rights.

However, they will almost always attend board meetings, give information and advice to the board, and have an opportunity to provide their views on any decisions that are being considered.

Part of the CEO's role is therefore to report to the board on the activities of the charity, advise them in their deliberations and carry out their wishes in relation to the running of the organisation.

Working with a board of trustees can be the most challenging part of the CEO's role. This is because boards consist of many folk from different backgrounds, with different expectations and interpretations of the work of the charity, and different levels of understanding. Although, technically, the chair should manage the board, in reality they will usually have their own other roles to fulfil. In practical terms, then, quite a bit of your CEO's time will be taken up with making sure that the members of the board have all the information they need, are operating at the right strategic level and are complying with their governance duties.

In whatever time they have left, the CEO's job is to make the rest of the organisation work! In broad terms, this means that CEOs:

- work with the other managers and directors to put plans in place to achieve the vision, mission and objectives of the charity;
- ensure that the charity's staff and volunteers have the resources and tools they need to carry out their work, within the parameters of what the charity can afford;
- ensure that the charity's finances are stable and sustainable;
- act as the public face of the charity – i.e. as the key spokesperson;
- on behalf of the board, make sure that the charity has all the appropriate policies, procedures, rules, regulations and practices in place to ensure it is complying with its legal and fiscal obligations.

The CEOs in many larger organisations may sometimes seem a bit remote from the everyday operations, simply because of the number of staff and volunteers working on the ground. More specifically, because of the size of the organisation, they have to rely heavily on information from the senior management team and trust that the managers and directors are implementing agreed plans and actions as well as complying with the charity's rules and regulations and its values. CEOs will usually have a broad overview of the work of the whole charity and will not necessarily be experts in any one particular area. Indeed, they shouldn't be, as they need to trust their managers and staff to do their jobs.

Directors and senior managers

Directors and senior managers normally have functional responsibilities for a certain area of the organisation. For example, they might be director of outreach programmes, finance director, director of fundraising and marketing, and so on. They will be accountable to the CEO for ensuring that their bit of the organisation delivers on its part of the overall plans. They will have a great deal of influence over the strategic direction of the organisation in terms of plans, priorities and general organisational culture.

Directors and senior managers are heavily dependent upon the work done and information provided to them by middle managers and/or team leaders. They work closely with the CEO to ensure that the plans and strategies that the board has agreed are implemented. These people will usually have a fairly high degree of freedom to decide how to implement the plans, and the good ones will work hard to ensure that their direct reports are involved in deciding how to get the work done.

There isn't one type of person who fits the senior manager role. Typically, however, the people at this level are a mixture of ambitious individuals interested in the top job and experienced people who don't necessarily want to progress further but enjoy the responsibility that comes with a senior position.

Middle managers

Middle management positions are usually only found in larger organisations. In smaller organisations, senior managers normally carry out the tasks that would be done by middle managers.

Middle managers are often in quite a vulnerable position, sandwiched between the senior levels (on the one hand) and the front line and team leaders (on the other). They are less likely than those higher up to be fully aware of the bigger picture and may sometimes feel left out of the loop. In my experience, they have a particularly tough job with a lot of responsibility, but often not much freedom to go with it. Even in charities!

Their job is usually to manage the team leaders and/or specialists of their departments and to carry out the directions of the more senior managers in the organisation. They are somewhat remote from the front line, as there will usually be team leaders in between them and the other staff.

Team leaders

This management level probably includes you! You will be accountable for a team with a very specific remit, usually focused on day-to-day operational issues. It is through you that much of the core work of the organisation will get done. You will have some level of authority over decision-making. You will be much closer to your beneficiaries, client base and/or service users than any of the other managers in the organisation. You will be uniquely placed to have a deep understanding of the issues involved in serving them and what works and doesn't work. You may not feel powerful but, believe me, you are!

If you are not effective in your role, the whole organisation suffers because you are at the core of the delivery of the work of the organisation. Only through you can all the strategic decisions reach the people who operate the machinery, drive the van, administer the medication, counsel the client, care for the patient, process the invoice, send out the funding application, organise the event ...

The difference between managers and other staff in practice

At all levels, from team leaders to directors, managers should support the decisions and strategies agreed upon by management. You must support the management line even if you don't agree with it. The reasons are obvious when you think about it. Firstly, the management appointed you, so casting its judgement into doubt by being publicly negative or cynical about managers' decisions is effectively casting doubt on their judgement when they appointed you! Secondly, and more importantly, if you undermine the management, you undermine your team and the rest of the organisation. This doesn't mean that you can't share your point of view with others; however, it means that you share it up the line, not down the line. This might sometimes feel like you're keeping your team out of the loop, but doing so won't damage your credibility with your team as long as you manage the situation sensitively and ensure that your team members understand that your role is to deliver for the organisation and not to be their shop steward.

Another thing that defines you as a manager is that you are accountable for the performance of others. What this means in practice is that, even if it wasn't your fault, you carry the can for the performance and, indeed, behaviour of your team members. You no longer get to say 'it wasn't my fault – it was so and so's' when you are the leader of the team. You are expected to be able to manage both the performance and the behaviour of others such that the job gets done well and there is relative harmony within the team and the organisation. If you don't, then your performance will be judged negatively.

'Eeeeek!', you may now be thinking, 'What have I done by taking this promotion?' Well, what you've done is given yourself the opportunity to help to grow and develop others, to play a key role in the work of your organisation and to learn new skills yourself. There will be tough times ahead for sure, but do you know what? It really is worth it.

Remember

1. The key part of your job is to make sure others do theirs well.
2. The technical or specialist aspect of your work is now secondary to your management of other folks' work.
3. You are part of a framework of managers and leaders, which means you will be expected to hold the management line.
4. Your role matters.

2 Making the transition: the first few weeks

'Where shall I begin, please your Majesty?' he asked. 'Begin at the beginning,' the King said, gravely, 'and go on till you come to the end; then stop.'
Lewis Carroll, *Alice's Adventures in Wonderland*

Whatever route you've taken to become a new manager – starting afresh in a new organisation, being promoted to a different department in the same organisation or moving up within your own department – you will undoubtedly be feeling a combination of nerves, excitement and anticipation. You're probably full of plans and ideas about how you want to do the job, what you want to change and so on.

Each of the routes to becoming a new manager is slightly different in terms of the challenges it presents. But, no matter how you got to where you are now, to avoid looking like a complete plank in the first few days and weeks, it helps if you have a sense of the organisational culture in which you will be starting out as a manager before you begin to implement any of your plans and ideas. Even if you think you already know the culture, it will feel different at management level.

Organisational cultures

All 'culture' means in this context is the implicit ways of working and interacting that the staff in an organisation have both with each other and with those they serve. Organisational cultures can be friendly or formal; flexible or rigid; open or bureaucratic. It is important to very quickly get a sense of how things work, as you will need to operate within the cultural norms, certainly in the early days, in order to get things done. Over time, you will have opportunities to influence the organisational culture. And, of course, you have a massive amount of influence over the culture within your own team. However, whatever cultures you encounter, if you approach your role with a visible and enthusiastic openness, you'll be OK.

Things to think about

In the following table I have suggested a few key things to consider about organisational cultures when starting off in your new role.

Consider	Establish	Suggestions
What is the culture of the organisation?	Is it strict and hierarchical? Is it relaxed and laissez-faire?	In the early days it's probably a good idea to follow the organisational rules, but, if the culture is generally a negative or cynical one, resist the temptation to get sucked into it just to fit in! If you don't feel you can challenge negativity in the early days, then your best approach is probably not to say anything until you have grown in confidence.
What is the expected dress code?	Are there things that you are expected to wear or not wear? Even if the staff tend to dress casually, do you notice the managers dressing more smartly?	Your outward appearance, especially in the early days, should not be a distraction for others. You can rebel later once you've settled into the role and are doing a good job! My advice is to err on the side of being smarter rather than more casual.

Is there a code of behaviour for managers?	Some organisations specify behaviours that are expected or not expected of managers. For example, at DSC we have a code which managers are expected to live up to.	If there isn't a specific code, there is nothing to stop you deciding for yourself the management and leadership behaviours you would like to be known for and adopting them from the get-go. The trick is to be consistent.

The three routes into management

I've already spoken about the various ways you can end up being promoted to a management position. The route that you take will have an influence on how you are perceived, and each route has its own challenges and positives.

New role, new organisation

This may well be your first foray into management and in the context of a brand-new organisation that you haven't worked for before. This can be both a blessing and a curse. Below I highlight some of the pros and cons of this situation and how you can play them to your advantage.

Pros	Cons	Playing the advantage
They don't know you	They don't know you	You have the opportunity to start afresh
They don't have any negative expectations	They don't have any positive expectations	You can decide from day one what kind of image you would like to project
You bring new ideas to the team	You have no history with the team and therefore may not fully understand the rationales for what is done	You are better able to view dispassionately what works and what doesn't work

You can get to know them with an unbiased view	Because you don't know them, you may be fooled by first appearances	You can make up your own mind
They are more likely to accept new ideas from you because you have the glamour of outside experience	They may view your new ideas with suspicion because you don't understand the organisation or its culture	You can come in with lots of new ideas and bring your learning from your past experiences – you will see things with a fresh eye
Members of existing networks have no prior experience of you	Members of existing networks have no prior experience of you – you will have to tap into existing networks, which can be very hard to do	You can create new relationships and help to positively influence existing group dynamics

New role, same organisation, different team

In this instance, you have been promoted within the organisation but into a team you have not been part of before. You will be somewhat familiar with the team and its work but probably not know as much as you think you do. And it will be the same for your new team when it comes to thinking about what they already know about you.

Pros	Cons	Playing the advantage
You already understand the wider culture of the organisation	You have preconceived ideas and opinions and may therefore be less objective	You can create a sense of safety with members of the new team if you approach them positively and make them feel as if you're already on their side

The team members probably already know you or of you and this will save time building relationships	The team already knows of you by reputation and may be suspicious of you	You have the opportunity to surprise them and make them feel valued by you
The team may be more willing to listen to your ideas as they already know that you understand the organisation	They may be less inclined to listen to your ideas as they think they already know what you think	This is a fabulous opportunity to position yourself as a manager who listens to the team and then acts on their ideas rather than imposing your own
If there was a member of the team who applied for your new job and didn't get it, you have an opportunity to help develop a member of your team who has ambitions beyond their role	That same team member may feel resentment towards you	If you handle this situation well, you have the opportunity to win a powerful ally within the team (see more on this in 'Learning about your team' on page 21)

New role, same organisation, same team

Personally, I think the type of transitional management role where a manager moves upwards in the same team is one of the hardest to pull off. My very first leadership role was one where I was promoted from within the team. My teammates were very keen on my promotion and hugely supportive ... for about a month. Unfortunately for them, I approached the role much like a bull in a china shop and managed to make every single member of the team bitterly regret my appointment. In the end, I fixed the situation and we ended up being an incredibly high-performing team who got on really well and did great work – but I wouldn't recommend my path to becoming a good manager as a preferred route!

Pros	Cons	Playing the advantage
You already know everyone and have some idea of their strengths and weaknesses	You already know everyone so probably have preconceived ideas about what they will be like to manage	You have the opportunity to see your colleagues through new 'managerial' eyes and thus have a great chance to re-motivate and re-inspire them
You have a good understanding of the work of the team and know from personal experience what does and doesn't work well	You are so close to how the team worked in the past that it may be difficult to be objective or look at the work in a new way	You have the opportunity with a new role to look with fresh eyes at how things are done
You know who did and who didn't work well with the previous managers and the reasons why	You may be overinfluenced by either the positive or the negative aspects of the previous manager's style, which may make it harder to create your own approach	You know what they say behind the manager's back (you probably once joined in!) and will therefore know what to guard against
You have good access to internal networks within the organisation and the team	You are already known so it may be hard for existing networks to accept new behaviours from you in your new role	You can create a new persona by acknowledging the challenges at your new level and asking for help and support

You get the chance to lead your team and encourage them to develop	You have to stand back from the team and make hard decisions about people who may previously have been your friends	You have the chance to bring out the best in people and the team and to improve the performance of the team as a whole
You get to make decisions and take responsibility	You have to make the transition from being a member of the team to being the team manager, and this can be very difficult to do	You can use the team to help you in this transition by asking for their support to help you to be a great manager – this approach will also help to win them over

The upshot
Whichever of the three routes is the one you took, there are two things you need to do immediately:
1. Establish yourself as the manager of the team.
2. Establish your working protocols.

I will talk later in this chapter about how to do these two things.

First things first
But, before all of that, it's worth thinking about those things that you can do before your first day to ease your transition into the new post, regardless of whether you are new to the organisation or not. In fact, if you have been promoted from within, I'd suggest that you do your prep as if you were brand new to the organisation – you may find you discover things that you didn't previously know.

Don't be embarrassed about starting to prepare for your new role before you even begin. At worst, your colleagues will just think you're a bit over-enthusiastic (not necessarily a bad thing) and, at best, it will reinforce for them that management made the right decision in appointing you.

First, and most importantly, you hopefully already understand the vision, mission and strategic aims of the organisation, as you will have researched all that before your interview. But, even if you already know these, it's worth reminding yourself of what they are. After all, you will partly be responsible for delivering them!

Next, in order to get off to a good start, try these things:

- Ask for copies of minutes, plans and other relevant documents, including personnel files, which you can read in your own time before you actually start the job. That way, you will have a head start.
- Ask for copies of all policies and procedures and familiarise yourself with them. These will be your go-to guides for the future in the organisation, so make sure you know what they are. You don't need to memorise them; you just need to know which documents exist and to have read through them to get a general sense of how they can help you.
- Make sure you are familiar with the whole work of the organisation, not just your own team's. Trawl the organisation's website and get to know what it does and how it presents itself to the public. Read the last two annual reports and accounts and any documents on the website that will tell you more about the way the organisation thinks and what its priorities are.
- Suggest meeting your team off-site before your first day, perhaps informally for a coffee or over a sandwich. The only purpose of this is for the members of the team to get to know you. Make it clear that it's not compulsory but just a way of giving them an opportunity to meet you and find out a bit about you before you start. They might think it a bit odd, but they will appreciate it in the long run. And, from your perspective, it will make your first day a little less intimidating.
- Give your new team members a copy of your CV before you start so they know a bit about your background and experience. This is all about establishing your credibility.
- Find out whether anyone from within the team applied for the role – you will need to get them onside (see 'Learning about your team' on page 21).

Induction

Ideally, your induction should begin before you even start the job. You should be given a plan even if you have been promoted from within the team. However, many organisations are not particularly good at getting inductions right, so, if they haven't prepared a plan for you, then prepare one for yourself.

These are the things you will need to know in order to be effective:

- your terms and conditions of employment, which may have changed now you are on the management ladder;
- the organisation's disciplinary and grievance procedures, which are especially important – you are now accountable for the performance of your staff and you are very likely to have to implement or follow these procedures at some point;
- the fire and security procedure, as you are accountable for your team's welfare and safety;
- information about the organisation's health and safety policy – again, you are now accountable for your staff's safety and well-being;
- any guidelines, such as dress codes, lunch periods and so on;
- protocols on use of the telephone, email, internet and post.

The first day

Don't try to do too much on day one. Getting yourself familiar with the basics – such as where the stationery is and how the phones and photocopiers work – is a really good use of time.

You should ask for time with your own line manager on the first day to clarify their expectations of you, the limits of your authority and your immediate priorities. It is as important for you to have a good relationship with your boss as it is for you to have good relationships with your team. Your job will be much harder if you don't invest time in getting your own boss's support.

Establish yourself as the manager of the team

One thing I particularly recommend you do on day one is to gather all of your team together and introduce yourself as the new manager. Ideally, you will let them all know before you start that this is what you would like to do, perhaps by making a call to someone in the team to let them know your intentions and agreeing a convenient time.

Either way, your introduction doesn't need to be long, but you should aim to cover the following:

- a brief account of your background: where you are from and what your experience is;
- some comments about why you took the job and why you think the organisation is important;
- how you plan to get to know the team and their work.

It's also worth asking your team members what their expectations are of you.

The best way to do this is face to face with all members of the team together. However, it is possible that your team is spread about. Again, you should still try to meet everybody in person, even if that means having to travel and spread your introductions over a couple of weeks.

You should do this even if you have been promoted from within the team. In fact, if anything, it's even more important in this case because you need to draw a line between being a member of the team and now being its manager.

I've drafted a form of words in the following box which might help you to decide exactly what to say. Of course, the wording is quite formulaic and perhaps a bit formal, so you will need to think about your own approach and style and use words that feel right for you, certainly if you have been promoted from within the team, because you will need to acknowledge that fact. I recommend you make a list of your key points so that you don't forget what it is you want to say.

Example introductory wording
Good morning, everyone. I've met some of you already and to those of you who I haven't met yet – hello.
I just wanted to gather you together briefly to say a few words.

Set the scene by making them feel good about themselves
Firstly, thank you for the welcome you've extended to me so far. It's always nerve-wracking coming to a new job and it helps when the team members are as warm and welcoming as you have been. (*It's worth saying this even if it isn't entirely true of the whole team as it creates an expectation from you to them about their behaviour for the future.*) And I'm already quite impressed by what I see. This makes me feel very encouraged about how well we will be able to work together.

Tell them a little bit about you
A little bit of background about me (*here, very briefly, describe what your previous job was and outline your general background – for example, that you have always been in finance; say something too about your personal circumstances – for example, married or not, kids or not, hobbies*).

Make them feel proud of the organisation and see that you are looking forward to working with them
I'm really pleased to have got this job. I've always admired (*name of organisation*) because (*why?*).

Let them know that you will spend time getting to know them and their work
I intend to spend my first couple of weeks getting to know you all and the work that you do, so I'll spend some time with each of you individually and we'll also spend some time together as a team.

Create expectations about how you want them to interact with you
I would like you to be frank and honest with me about the problems that you face and what things you think we could do to make our work easier

and more effective. The more open you are with me, the easier it will be for me to help us to resolve issues.

Ask for their help
I would like to be a good leader for you so I will be asking you all what it is you think I can do to help you as individuals and what I can do to help the team be the best it can be.

Whatever you decide to say, *do not* avoid some sort of introduction of the kind suggested above. It helps to establish you as the new manager, sets the tone for the first few weeks of your leadership and, if you handle it well, helps to ease your transition. As I emphasised earlier, do this even if you have been promoted from within the team. It will probably feel a bit strange, but you need to do something to mark the fact that you are now in a different role and you are not a member of the team in the way you were before. Some folk may mock you for doing it. If they do, so be it. You'll need to get used to getting knocked by the team anyhow – that's part of the job description!

Learning about your team
The best way to learn about the members of your team is to listen to them. That means taking the time to find out about their jobs, what they do, what they like and dislike about their work, and so on. This is particularly important in relation to anyone who may have applied for your role and been disappointed. In this case, you can win them over by asking their advice and testing your thinking on them. What are their thoughts on how you're planning to deal with a tricky customer problem? What performance indicators would they suggest you use to monitor a crucial team project? Make them feel knowledgeable, involved and important – because they are.

Arrange one-to-ones with every single member of the team. Allow at least an hour for each of these first meetings and have them at a location away from the team's work space. I always think one-to-ones are best held off-site over a coffee or a sandwich, the reason being that I have found that folk are more relaxed off-site in a neutral environment and are more likely to be open, self-reflective and honest. I'd avoid having one-to-ones in your office (if you have one) because that reinforces the hierarchical gap between you and the members of your team, which may not be conducive to building great relationships – certainly in the early days. At any rate, find a private place. It will be hard for your team members to be completely open with you if they think their colleagues can overhear them. At this point, they are likely to care more about what their colleagues think about them than what you think about them, and they will probably not want to come across as a brown-noser or traitor to the rest of the team by being too friendly with you.

In your first one-to-one with each team member, your main objective should be to understand exactly what the person does. What is their job and how does it contribute to the team's objectives? What are the challenges of their job? What are the problems and the frustrations? And what do they enjoy about their job? Which are the best bits?

Also take the time to find out what their key relationships are with the rest of the organisation. Whom do they work most closely with outside the immediate team? Which other departments do they have issues with? And so on. This helps to give you a wider context in which to understand their work and how well they do it.

Additionally, of course, you will want to learn a bit about each team member personally: their hopes, dreams, ambitions, fears and so on. You have to remember that people in the workplace are not independent of their personal relationships and it matters that you understand the wider context of the human being you are about to manage. Having said that, bear in mind that some people might not be willing to open up, or at least not immediately, so you should approach any personal matters with care.

At this stage of getting to know the members of your team, you shouldn't be making any promises about what you will or won't change – it's probably too soon, as you will need to see the whole picture and hear from everyone before you start changing things. By letting team members share their frustrations with you, however, you are building up a picture of them, of the rest of the team and of the work generally. And they are bound to have good ideas about what could be made better.

I would also recommend in these first one-to-ones that you ask them what they want of you as their manager and what support you can offer them in their work. Again, don't make any promises – just listen and note what they say. As they probably haven't been asked this before, it will be a way of showing them that you're open to them giving you feedback in the future. It will also give you an idea of what sort of leadership and management they are looking for.

'Walking the job'

Learning about the people in your team is about much more than private one-to-ones. You need to do what I call 'walking the job' – in other words, get off your pretty behind and go to your team members. Don't make the mistake of thinking that, just because their desks are only a few feet away from yours, you know what's going on. The reality is that people generally find it much easier to say what's on their mind if you are in their territory – where they feel comfortable, safe and at home. Make walking the job a habit that you carry on doing throughout your management life – whatever level you get to.

Your resources versus their resources

This is a very personal view; however, I am firmly of the belief that, as a manager, your job is to look after your people before you look after yourself by ensuring that they have the best available resources. There is nothing that causes more resentment within the team than when the manager has the best desk, the best computer, the only chair that isn't broken (in a charity there are always broken chairs!) and the best spot by the window. In terms of where you sit, the ideal spot is where you can see and be seen by others. If you aren't required to have your own office, then I suggest you don't. In my experience, you and your team will be much more effective if you can see and hear each other.

Reinforce your new role as the manager of the team

I have already spoken about establishing yourself formally as the manager of the team in that first meeting. However, there are other things that you can do to ensure that your team members understand you are the new boss.

First, as soon as you receive information that the team needs to know, either from your own boss or from others, gather people around and let them know – this is because, in my experience, people have a tendency to attribute credibility to the people who have access to information which they then share. If someone other than you is telling them what's going on, they are more likely to look to that person for leadership than to you.

Second, if someone in the team asks you to make a decision, then make it, but make sure you have asked their opinion first. (See also 'Decision-making in groups' on page 66 about the importance of allowing members of the team to make their own decisions as often as possible.)

Establish your working protocols

What I mean by establishing your working protocols is that you need to agree with your team what is expected from them in terms of keeping you informed about what's going on, what's happening with their work and so on – the working ground rules, if you like. What these rules are will depend on what you and the team decide. The rules might cover things such as:

- what to do if any of your team members have a problem;
- what you expect to be informed about and what you don't need to know about;
- what decisions team members can make themselves and which you need to be involved with;
- how you plan to communicate with the team – when you are happy for email to be used and when you want conversations to happen face to face, for example;
- when team meetings will be, how often and so on;
- how often team members will have one-to-ones and what you expect them to prepare for the meeting.

Get some training

No matter how experienced or competent you think you are, you really do need to organise some management and leadership training for yourself. Do not make the mistake of thinking that you will automatically know what to do in any given circumstances. Management is a skill like any other and, even if you're naturally gifted, you will need some help and advice to hone your technique.

If your organisation can't afford to send you for training, there are a number of very good management books out there which may help (see 'Recommended reading' on page 128). Either way, no matter how well prepared you are going into the new role, you will inevitably make mistakes. Don't freak out about them! They are unlikely to be doozies. Apologise and move on, and you'll be fine.

Remember

1. Do your homework. Make sure you understand the implicit and explicit rules and behaviours of the organisation and team.
2. Introduce yourself properly as the new manager.
3. Ask for training.

3 Your role as leader

A good leader inspires people to have confidence in the leader; a great leader inspires people to have confidence in themselves.
Unknown

Once you are in a management role, you will start to hear people talking about you as a leader. You might find yourself feeling a little confused about what the difference is between a manager and a leader – or whether there actually is one. Well, there is. Management is the term that describes the actions you take around *things*, and leadership is the term that describes the actions you take around *people*. Yet, while management and leadership are not the same thing, they are two sides of the same coin.

The following table broadly breaks down how I see the difference.

Managers	Leaders
Plan	Dream
Analyse	Imagine
Motivate	Inspire
Set objectives	Create vision
See people as resources	See people as people
Act tactically	Think strategically
Think 'what?'	Think 'why?'

In each of these pairs of actions, neither one is better than its counterpart. You need to have skills from both sides in order to lead and manage your team or organisation effectively.

In fact, lacking either of the two types of skill will cause huge problems in your ability to deliver against your objectives. There is absolutely no point having a big dream unless you have a plan to achieve it. And yes, in one sense people are resources and they are in a job to accomplish goals, but you get the best out of people when you treat them as human beings working alongside you.

Indeed, I've had experience of the extremes of these two sides of the coin. I once worked for a manager who was absolutely inspirational. He had a knack of making you feel you could achieve the impossible. Unfortunately, though, he was terrible at basic management, so we had no clear objectives and no way of knowing whether we were doing what we needed to do to achieve the impossible. So guess what? We didn't achieve it.

I worked for another guy who was a brilliant manager. For example, when you had a one-to-one with him he knew in detail how you were doing against your targets, and he would be very clear and specific about future tasks. But, when push came to shove, it all seemed a bit pointless – what were we doing all this stuff for? In this case, we didn't achieve the bigger vision either, because the manager was unable to inspire in us an understanding of *why* it all mattered – and why we mattered.

In both scenarios, the outcome was the same: we failed to meet the objective and we felt demotivated. So you do need both skills to complement each other.

However, I am going to concentrate on leadership for two reasons – firstly, because it's probably the harder part and, secondly, because we are generally taught how to plan, analyse, set objectives and so on. In other words, management skills are relatively easy to learn and implement. But knowing how to dream? How to inspire? How to think strategically? This is much harder stuff and usually not something we get training on.

When I was new to management roles, my colleagues and I were frequently told on management training courses a funny (but not true) story that illustrated how easy it is for organisations to confuse leadership and management and therefore completely miss the real problem.

A story about the difference between management and leadership

Two companies – Bloated Industries Ltd and Workcorp Inc. – decided to hold a competitive staff boat race on the River Thames. Workcorp Inc. won the first race by a mile. Bloated Industries Ltd became discouraged and morale at the company sagged. Senior managers decided the reason for this defeat had to be found, so they set up an internal project team to investigate the cause and recommend appropriate action.

The resulting report identified that Workcorp Inc. team had eight people rowing and one person steering. Bloated Industries Ltd, in contrast, had one person rowing and eight people steering. Senior management at Bloated Industries Ltd hired a consultant to study their company team's structure. Several months later, the consultant concluded in a leather-bound report that too many people were steering and not enough were rowing.

An action plan was immediately put into place to prevent Workcorp Inc. from winning again. Bloated Industries Ltd team's structure was changed to four rowing managers, three senior rowing managers, an executive rowing manager and a rower. A performance and appraisal system was set up to give the person rowing the boat more incentive to work harder and become a top performer.

Workcorp Inc. won the next race by an increased margin of two miles. Bloated Industries Ltd reacted by halting development work on the new boat and laying off the rower due to their poor performance. They gave a high-performance award to the consultant and distributed the rest of the money made to senior management.

I'm sure that you immediately see the irony and humour in this story. It is made up, of course, but it probably resonates a little. The aim of the story is not to belittle structures and the important role of managers but to make the point that managers themselves can sometimes miss the point! The purpose of management is to serve the workers so that they can serve others. Not the other way around.

Leadership models

I've found that there are as many models of leadership as there are colours of paint! Yet, despite the massive amount of information out there, I always recommend reading about leadership as widely as you can.

From a purely practical point of view, however, there are three models which I think cover all of the bases and are simple to both understand and implement: action-centred leadership, liberating leadership and outstanding leadership.

Action-centred leadership

Action-centred leadership was developed by John Adair. He based this approach on considerable research into what makes leaders most effective and I like it particularly for two reasons. Firstly, because it is simple and easy to follow; secondly, because it maps some of what you need to be doing from both the management and the leadership perspective.

The action-centred leadership approach suggests that your personal traits – character, background, education and so on – are irrelevant. Instead, it is what leaders *do* – their actions and behaviour – that matters, not who they are or what they know.

The action-centred leadership model

The model describes the three elements of your role: you need to get the job done, you need to make sure your people have the right skills and motivation to get it done, and you need the team to work together.

This model also demonstrates that, although there are actions that are specific to each part of your role, they overlap. If you focus on one part of the circle at the expense of the others, you will not achieve your objectives.

The Three Circles © John Adair

The five key stages

You can use the following five key stages to apply this model of leadership.

1. Define your objectives

You need to be really clear about what it is you are trying to achieve and the context in which that effort takes place – i.e. the 'why' of the activity. The job may be about banking cheques, for example, but there is a context for that job, such as the organisation's need to ensure it has plenty of cash in the bank in order to pay its bills so that it can do its work.

This means you need to be clear about the purpose of your own job, the purpose of the team and how both of these fit into the overall purpose of the organisation.

2. Plan

Once you are clear about what needs to be done and why, you need to make sure that you have an appropriate plan of action. People often believe that plans need to be lengthy documents full of graphs, statistics and diagrams. Not so. The written plan is not the key thing – the act of planning is what actually matters. However, having a visual representation of your plan is a demonstration of the fact that you have thought about how to go about doing what needs to be done, factoring in the resources you will need to do it. This reassures people and helps you to remember what you have decided to do.

Make sure during this phase that you are really listening to people and what they are telling you. Firstly, they will undoubtedly have access to information and/or resources that you don't. Secondly, if you have involved people in your thinking at the early stages, they are much more likely to support whatever the final plan is (even if they don't entirely agree with it) because they will have felt involved.

And, remember, things will never go according to the plan. The plan is a map, not a railway track. You can, and probably should, deviate from it when required.

3. Brief and communicate

Remember the saying 'there's many a slip 'twixt cup and lip'? In my experience, the slip is normally either that we forget to brief people about what the plans and actions are or that we don't realise how important it is to get this bit of communication right. As a result, we don't prioritise it and don't give it appropriate attention. It is vital to let people know what's going on and what will be happening.

4. Monitor and support

Coming up with the plans is the easy part! The hard part is supporting people in delivering against them. And using the terms 'monitor' and 'support' rather than 'check' matters. The term 'check' implies a lack of trust, whereas 'monitor' and 'support' imply trust with back-up.

Anyone doing a job, even if it's not the first time they've done it, is going to make mistakes. At the risk of sounding clichéd, mistakes are important because that's how we learn what works and what doesn't work, and how we can improve. Both penicillin and Post-it Notes were the results of mistakes. As Thomas Edison apocryphally said, he didn't fail 10,000 times but rather he succeeded in proving 10,000 ways how *not* to build a light bulb. Imagine if he'd given up at number 9,999!

But how do you monitor and support without making people feel that you're checking up on them? Well, tell them that you will be monitoring how they get on with their job so that, if they get stuck or face difficulties, you will be able to help them. Saying things like 'I'll pop over to see you on Friday to see how you're getting on and if you need any help' does not upset people; it means that they're expecting you and they get the context of your scrutiny.

And do remember, it's part of your job as a manager to actively look for things that are being done right as well as those things that aren't going so well!

5. Evaluate

Remembering to evaluate is a bit like remembering the sky is blue – we so often forget to look up that we don't notice it is. And we often forget to review what we have been doing to see what worked, what didn't work and what we could do differently or better next time. Don't skip this step. It's easy to evaluate when a project went wrong and much harder to remember to take the time to evaluate when it went right. And yet understanding what you did well is just as useful as working out why things didn't go so well.

A simple toolbox

Below is a simple framework that outlines, under the headings of task, team and individual, the actions that you need to do to fulfil your management and leadership roles effectively. Think of this as a toolbox: if there is any area that you feel is not working, have a look at this table and you will instantly see either the action you need to do again or the stage you omitted. Then all you have to do is put it right.

For more on each of the three areas (individual, team and task), see chapters 4, 5, and 6, respectively.

Key actions		Task	Team	Individual
Define objectives		Identify tasks and constraints	Hold team meetings; share commitment	Clarify objectives; gain acceptance
Plan	Gather information	Consider options Check resources	Consult Develop suggestions Encourage ideas Assess skills	
	Decide	Priorities Timescales Standards	Structure	Allocate tasks Delegate Set targets
Brief		Clarify objectives Describe plan	Explain decisions Answer questions Check understanding	Listen Enthuse
Monitor and support		Co-ordinate Assess progress Maintain standards	Advise Reconcile conflict	Assist Reassure Counsel (coach) Discipline
Evaluate		Summarise Review objectives Replan if necessary	Recognise and gain from success Learn from mistakes	Appraise performance
			Guide, train and give praise	

Adapted from *The Manager as a Leader*, Industrial Society Press, 1989.

In summary, action-centred leadership is essentially the *doing* part of leadership and management. It gives you the basic tools you need to get the job done, build your team and develop individuals.

However, I believe there is an important ingredient not covered here. And that's about the *being* part of leadership. Although you can do all of the above key actions regardless of the type of person you are, it is my experience that the kind of person you are can have a huge effect on how well you do them.

Liberating leadership

Back in the 1990s, when I worked for an organisation called the Industrial Society (now the Work Foundation), my colleagues and I did a huge analysis of what modern leadership was about. We surveyed thousands of employees and their managers to find out what made a team member want to follow the leader. The result of this extended research was the development of a concept called liberating leadership.

Liberating leadership turns the word 'leader' into an acronym as follows:

L	**Liberate**	Free those people closest to the job to make their own decisions – keep interference and direction to a minimum
E	**Encourage and support**	Spend a great deal of time enthusing and encouraging staff and building up their belief in their abilities
A	**Achieve the purpose**	Get the job done: make sure that the objectives are clear and that people know what to do – and celebrate when it's done
D	**Develop people and teams**	Give people responsibility: make sure they are well trained and supported; take as many opportunities as you reasonably can to generate a team culture
E	**Set an example**	Make sure your own behaviour reflects the behaviour you would like to see in your staff
R	**Build relationships through trust**	Make it clear that you trust people by listening to them and acting on their advice; give them opportunities to shine

As you can see, there are similarities between this model and that of action-centred leadership. However, the key difference is that the liberating leadership model also asks leaders to learn about the needs, values and motivations of staff and to use this knowledge to free them up to achieve.

Outstanding leadership
Outstanding leadership is another model of leadership; it focuses more on the emotional connection that leaders should have with their people and their work. In 2010, the Work Foundation published a report on the principles of outstanding leadership.

The research analysed the difference between good leadership and outstanding leadership as follows:

Good	Outstanding
■ Objectives and targets ■ Act due to beliefs and values ■ Focus on skill ■ Delegate task ■ Believe leader holds responsibility ■ Involvement in vision and strategy ■ Give time to others ■ Tend to focus on work ■ Vision as clarity of purpose ■ Focus on team structure and location ■ Give a good impression ■ Reflect on learning about the job ■ People and task important ■ WYSIWYG (what you see is what you get) ■ Develop through learning and coaching ■ Use systems and procedures ■ Attend to many things	■ People and engagement ■ Act due to consequences ■ Focus on attitude and engagement ■ Delegate space for autonomy ■ Want team to own responsibility ■ Co-creation of vision and strategy ■ Focus on people as route to success ■ Seek to understand people and motives ■ Vision as emotional clarion call ■ Focus on team cohesion and equality ■ Reflect on symbolic role of leadership ■ Reflect on learning about self and others ■ People at centre – task through people ■ Consistent and careful with their behaviour ■ Develop through challenge and support ■ Focus on key procedures to reduce burden ■ Emphasis on people first then move on to focusing on tasks

Differences between good and outstanding leaders, adapted from *Exceeding Expectations: The principles of outstanding leadership – Executive summary.*

The authors then identified three principles of outstanding leaders:
1. They think and act systemically:
   - They see the bigger picture.
   - They understand how things connect to each other and influence each other.
   - They understand that trust and confidence help people to be creative and effective.

2. They see people as the route to performance:
   - They focus on people and relationships.
   - They spend a lot of time listening to people.
   - They understand that people feeling capable and engaged helps to achieve high performance.
3. They are self-confident without being arrogant:
   - They are highly self-aware.
   - They realise that it is their own behaviour, rather than the effect of systems and procedures, that will influence people's performance.
   - They are driven to achieve the purpose, not personal glory.

The following table outlines the nine characteristics of outstanding leaders:

Outstanding leaders	
Characteristic	*What this means in practice*
Think systemically and act with the long term in mind	See both the bigger picture and the long-term goal
Bring meaning to life	Communicate an inspiring vision and the organisation's purpose
Apply the spirit not the letter of the law	Use minimal systems and processes and focus on outcomes
Are self-aware and put themselves in others' shoes	Understand themselves and others
Understand that talk is work	Take time to listen to people
Give time and space to others	Spend time with people
Grow people through performance	Create opportunities for responsibility and growth
Put 'we' before 'me'	Focus on team values, share responsibility for decision-making and put their own needs second
Take deeper breaths and hold them longer	Develop trust and give people freedom to fail

Adapted from 'Nine themes that characterise outstanding leaders' in *Exceeding Expectations: The principles of outstanding leadership*

I think this model is a useful one because it helps you to think about your values and attitudes as a leader, not just your actions. Which leads me nicely onto the next point: you as a leader.

What's your leadership style?

The models I've described so far are all useful for thinking about how you might behave in certain situations. It's also important, though, to have a good understanding of what your own natural leadership style is and how that might affect the people you are leading.

You must have noticed that there are some managers whom some team members think are awful and other team members think are great. Many years ago I worked for a CEO whom I thought was a great leader. I didn't think he was perfect, but I really admired his leadership style and I learned an enormous amount from him which I am still applying today. I would still say he was one of the best leaders I worked for. However, one of my colleagues, and in fact a close friend of mine, had a completely different view of him and was not a fan at all. So what was the difference? Why did she see him so differently from the way I did? From what I could observe, he didn't seem to treat her any differently from how he treated me.

Over time, I've come to realise that the answer is, of course, that we were perceiving the same person very differently. I believed that one of this CEO's strengths was that he was behaviourally very consistent. He treated us all exactly the same. But I have since come to realise that the fact that he was so consistent was probably part of the problem. His natural style very much fitted in with my personality and how I like to do things. He was decisive and quick-thinking so things moved quickly – a style similar to my own. My colleague, on the other hand, was very cerebral, a deep thinker and profoundly academically clever. I think that she struggled with his leadership style because it gave her the impression that he didn't think things through properly. I think, perhaps, he occasionally experienced her as obstructive because he thought she wanted to slow things down and he couldn't see the reason why; at the same time, she saw him as reckless because he wanted to get on with it, but she felt he wasn't taking the time to properly consider the situation. I don't think either of them was wrong, but I do now suspect that if he had been more open to adapting his style to my colleague's way of thinking, they would probably have both benefitted.

So, the issue of leadership style is an important one. It isn't about deciding that you have a style and that's it – others just have to suck it up and get on with it. It's about recognising that actually what you are trying to do as a leader is to get people to follow you. If you start with that as a premise, you will do what it takes to get them following you. That doesn't mean you are being inauthentic at all. What it means is that you are being sensitive to the people you are leading, to their needs and to the ways in which they best respond to leadership.

This approach is the behavioural equivalent of wearing the right clothes at the right time. You wouldn't wear a bikini to a funeral or a suit to the beach. Similarly, you wouldn't rush people who need more time and, with those who need quicker responses, you'd just get on with it.

If you are finding some team members challenging, it may, of course, be that they're just awkward sods, but it's equally likely that they simply don't respond well to your particular leadership style. The answer? Put their needs first and adapt your style, of course!

To adapt your style, however, you need to understand it. I developed the following leadership style test for charity CEOs, but I think it applies equally to anyone in a leadership position. There are no right or wrong answers; one style is not better than another. It is simply a tool to get you to think – do not use it to label yourself or others! The sole purpose of the test is to make you review the relationships you have with those you lead and to consider how you can adapt your own style to get the best out of those relationships.

Leadership style test

Instructions

Look at one row at a time. Thinking about yourself in a leadership context, give each word a value from **1** to **4** with **4** representing the word most like you and **1** representing the word least like you. You must have one of each number only in every row so that each row adds up to 10. In other words, every line must contain a **4**, a **3**, a **2**, and a **1**.

Example

	Score		Score		Score		Score
Funny	4	**Interesting**	2	**Quiet**	1	**Determined**	3

The test

	Score		Score		Score		Score
Trusting		**Precise**		**Enthusiastic**		**Quick**	
Confident		**Supportive**		**Careful**		**Creative**	
Imaginative		**Forceful**		**Responsive**		**Economical**	
Methodical		**Demonstrative**		**Competitive**		**Helpful**	
Determined		**Persuasive**		**Analytical**		**Receptive**	
Adaptable		**Practical**		**Encouraging**		**Courageous**	
Objective		**Empathetic**		**Inspiring**		**Animated**	
Generous		**Strong-willed**		**Mischievous**		**Factual**	
Focused		**Relaxed**		**Challenging**		**Experimental**	
Fun		**Action-oriented**		**Relationship focused**		**Questioning**	

Once you have completed this test, copy your score from the original sheet onto this next sheet. The sheet uses codes that indicate four coloured categories: red is R, green is G, blue is B and yellow is Y. The colours have been chosen on the basis of associations between them and the words used in the test (each colour represents a theme which will be introduced below).

		Score			Score			Score			Score
G	Trusting		B	Precise		Y	Enthusiastic		R	Quick	
R	Confident		G	Supportive		B	Careful		Y	Creative	
Y	Imaginative		R	Forceful		G	Responsive		B	Economical	
B	Methodical		Y	Demonstrative		R	Competitive		G	Helpful	
R	Determined		Y	Persuasive		B	Analytical		G	Receptive	
Y	Adaptable		B	Practical		G	Encouraging		R	Courageous	
B	Objective		G	Empathetic		R	Inspiring		Y	Animated	
G	Generous		R	Strong-willed		Y	Mischievous		B	Factual	
B	Focused		G	Relaxed		R	Challenging		Y	Experimental	
Y	Fun		R	Action-oriented		G	Relationship focused		B	Questioning	

Now add up each score under each colour – all the reds, all the yellows, all the blues and all the greens – and mark them in the chart below.

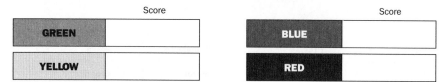

	Score			Score
GREEN			BLUE	
YELLOW			RED	

To check your scoring, make sure that no box adds up to more than 40 or less than 4.

You will probably find that you have a different score in each box. What this means is that the higher the score in any one particular area, the more characteristic those words are of your personal leadership style.

So, for example, if you scored highly in blue, you probably come across as thoughtful and detailed – someone who likes to take time to consider things properly. Which is fine. To those in your team who score highly in the red category, however, this approach is likely to be frustrating since they require less information before deciding and just want to get on with it.

You will notice that the words in each category have a common theme. So, for example:

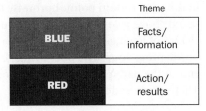

	Theme			Theme
GREEN	Feelings/ relationships		**BLUE**	Facts/ information
YELLOW	Ideas/ change		**RED**	Action/ results

Depending on what your team members' natural styles are, they may perceive your own style positively or negatively, as the chart below shows.

	When viewed positively, could be seen as:	*When viewed negatively, could be seen to be:*
GREEN **Feelings/ relationships**	■ Caring ■ Supportive ■ Interested in individuals ■ Nurturing ■ Interested in relationships ■ Warm ■ A good listener	■ Overly nurturing ■ Misplaced in their loyalties by prioritising individuals over the task ■ Not letting people grow or make their own mistakes ■ Hanging on to poor performers ■ Too soft
BLUE **Facts/ information**	■ Practical ■ Attentive to details ■ Getting the facts right ■ A clear, logical decision-maker ■ Authoritative ■ Thoughtful	■ Wanting too much order ■ Overly attentive to detail ■ Never getting anything done ■ Always playing by the rules ■ Closed-minded ■ Overly focused on facts
YELLOW **Ideas/ change**	■ Enthusiastic ■ Creative and prepared to experiment ■ Fun to work with ■ Open-minded ■ Ready to challenge the status quo ■ Looking for new possibilities	■ Addicted to change ■ Ineffective ■ Fickle – starting lots of initiatives all at once ■ Not getting results ■ Not seeing things through
RED **Action/ results**	■ Confident ■ Quick ■ Gets results ■ Dynamic ■ Focused ■ Inspiring	■ Only interested in action ■ Unconcerned about individuals ■ A bad listener ■ Bullying ■ Not thinking things through

The point is that none of these styles is the best or worst style for a leader – all it means is that you need to adapt your style depending on whom you are leading at a certain point. I promise that if you put the way *other people* need to be led above *your* need to lead in your natural style, you really do stand a better chance of having happy, productive team members who produce great work.

Adapting your style doesn't make it inauthentic – it's just behaviour, at the end of the day. You are treating people the way they would like to be treated. That's good leadership!

What's the upshot?

In summary, I believe the core messages from each of these leadership models can be broken down into two clear rules: **think within** and **act without**. Thinking within is about knowing yourself. Acting without is about how you manifest as a leader and deliver for your organisation and your team.

Think within

Thinking within is sort of like developing your own manifesto for what you will do and how you will be as a leader. It's about being really clear about your own values as a human being. What *really* matters to you? How do you know when you are living up to your values? What behaviours do you think you should be exhibiting?

It means knowing in which cases you are prepared to compromise your principles and values and when you are not willing to do so.

For example, you might have the following as your leadership principles:

- I believe that people matter more than processes.
- I believe that when I listen to understand I get better results from others.
- I believe that when I openly admit my own mistakes I unconsciously give others permission to do the same.

But thinking within is more than values, behaviours and principles. It's also these things:

- Know what your strengths and weaknesses are. Be neither falsely modest nor overly complacent; continually remind yourself of what you do well, so you can keep doing it, and of what you do less well, so you can keep working on improving it.
- Let go of your ego but hang on to your self-belief. Ego is the part of us that drives vanity-led decisions. Self-belief is the part of us that drives cause-led decisions.
- Remember: taken in the round, you are no better and no worse than almost any other human being on the planet. Give yourself permission to take risks and therefore to make mistakes, and permission to forgive yourself when you get it wrong – which you will.

Act without

Acting without is about how you manifest your beliefs about leadership and your approach to it with your team.

- Be clear what your vision is for the team or organisation. What will it look like if you succeed in your work?
- Communicate your vision: daily through your actions, weekly through your words and monthly through your written work.
- Trust others. Let them get it wrong, forgive them and give them another chance to get it wrong. (In other words, let folk fail. It's how they learn and how things improve.)
- Continually remind people of the purpose of the organisation.
- Frequently remind people of how they contribute to the overall purpose of the organisation.
- Put the needs of your people above your own – visibly and demonstrably.
- Act quickly and decisively to deal with poor or negative behaviour.
- Be quick to praise. Praise often and wholeheartedly – but keep it real.

I still think leadership is the hardest part of the role of a manager in many ways. You have to be constantly thinking about and evaluating your own behaviour and approach – on alert for how you might be getting it wrong – and you must be willing to make mistakes and to go back to fix them. However difficult it may be to be continually finding fault with your own actions, it is good to do so because it means that you are paying attention – you are noticing. And when you notice something you give yourself the possibility to be brilliant at it!

Remember

1. Management and leadership both matter.
2. Leadership is not only about *what* you do but also about *who* you are.
3. Notice what you are thinking, doing and saying, observe the effect it has on those around you and adapt your style accordingly.

4 Developing the talent

Treat people as if they were what they ought to be, and you help them become what they are capable of being.
Attributed to Johann Wolfgang von Goethe

By definition, the fact that you are a manager means that the task you have been asked to do is too big for one person. So you need others. This means recruiting and developing individuals to help you to achieve the task.

You are likely to inherit individuals in your team. However, there may be times when you get the opportunity to choose a new team member yourself. There is a myth that if you choose the people yourself, you will get the right ones. In my experience, unless you've previously worked with the person you are about to recruit, any appointment you make is a bit of a risk. You're making a judgement based on a CV, an interview and some references. For as many folk I've appointed where the decision was brilliant, there have been those whom I thought would be awesome but weren't. So don't blame the poor performance of a team member on the fact that you didn't choose them. It doesn't matter how they came to you – it's what you do with them that counts.

Getting the best out of people

In order for a plant to grow well, there are some basic things that it needs regardless of what type of plant it is. To thrive it needs the right soil, the right aspect, the right amount of nutrition and the appropriate amount of sunlight.

It's the same with people. Regardless of the person or the job, everyone needs to know these three things:
1. Who is my boss?
2. What is expected of me?
3. How will I know how well I am doing?

It may seem like the responses to these questions should be obvious, but you'd be surprised how often it is that people don't know the answers.

Who is my boss?

Everyone needs *one* person who is their ultimate boss – the person who carries out their one-to-ones, appraises their performance, gives them permission for holidays, and disciplines them if they are not performing and praises them if they are.

For an individual you manage, it may not always be obvious who the boss is, particularly if they work on multiple projects each with a different person who is senior to them. You need to be really clear in cases like these that you are the manager of that individual, regardless of who else they are working with or what else they are working on. You can always consult others when it comes to giving feedback on your direct reports' performance if they are working on things that you don't know much about – but, again, they need to know it's you who is their ultimate manager. Furthermore, you're the one who needs to step in to resolve conflicts of priority if they are being asked to do too many things at the same time by different people.

What is expected of me?

This is about clearly laying out a number of things:

- the key tasks that must be completed;
- the standard to which those tasks must be delivered;
- the approach and attitude that you expect to be taken towards delivering those tasks.

The first two are fairly straightforward, but you must make sure that the standards are very specific. Saying things like 'reports must be completed in a timely fashion' is meaningless. What does 'timely' mean? You need to be explicit – for example, 'reports must be completed within five working days of the end of the project'.

The third point – about approach and attitude – is particularly important. How people behave in the workplace matters, so you need to specify which behaviours are acceptable and which are not. For instance, complaining about another colleague is not acceptable. If one of your team members complains to you about a colleague, the first thing you need to do is to remind them that the outcome is likely to be much better if they can resolve the problem themselves, before involving you, and that you can coach them through doing so. Only if that doesn't work should they then come to you.

How will I know how well I am doing?

This is about ensuring that the team member knows the structures and processes that monitor performance. For example, you need to make sure that they:

- have regular one-to-ones where they know you will feed back on their performance to date;
- have the opportunity to ask questions or seek support;
- know how the performance management system works;
- know who gives input into appraisals.

As a manager, you must make sure that you are regularly spending time with your team members to reflect on their performance and work with them to help them be the best they can be.

Motivating people

> May I ask whether these pleasing attentions proceed from the impulse of the moment, or are the result of previous study?
>
> Jane Austen, *Pride and Prejudice*

I need to lay my cards on the table here. I do not believe that managers can motivate people. I believe that what managers can do is create an environment where people can motivate themselves.

What managers can absolutely do, however, is *demotivate* people. So, for me, motivation is more about the things you need to do (or not do) in order to *not* demotivate your people.

Characteristics of motivated, demotivated and unmotivated people

In my experience, there are three kinds of people: those who are **motivated**, those who are **demotivated** and those who are **unmotivated**. The first kind get on with it, the second kind complain about it and the third kind don't do much of anything at all!

I've broken down the classic characteristics of these three types of people in the table below so that you can identify where your team members might be. Of course, these are highly exaggerated versions of behaviour, but you'll get the gist.

Motivated	Demotivated	Unmotivated
Ask questions for clarification	Ask rhetorical questions which are unanswerable	Don't ask questions
Seek to solve problems	Point out problems to others	Ignore problems
Want to share knowledge and experience with others	Want to complain about difficulties to others	Don't talk about the task or job at all
Work hard to get on well with others	Complain about others	Largely ignore others
Put in the time to get the job done	Waste time	Do the bare minimum to get the job done

Are generally quick to respond to requests	Respond to requests reluctantly	Ignore requests
Seek to help others	Can't help others and don't ask for help themselves	Doesn't occur to them that they might need help or offer help
Generally seem positive	Generally seem negative	Are neither positive nor negative because they are disengaged from the task
Are more likely to cope with things going wrong with good humour	Are more likely to overreact to things going wrong or complain about them	Don't care if things go wrong
Have a positive attitude to problems – 'I can sort this out'	Have a negative attitude to problems – don't think they can sort it out	Ignore problems

Motivated people are easy to work with! You just let them get on with it and praise them regularly. It's the other kinds that are the hardest challenge.

Motivation theories which might help

There are many different theories of motivation. I have personally found the following two to be the most useful:

- Maslow's hierarchy of needs
- McGregor's Theory X and Theory Y

These theories are quite old, having been developed in the 1960s for the most part, but I personally have found them useful throughout my management career and believe much of the basic thinking is still relevant today.

Maslow's hierarchy of needs

Abraham Maslow was a psychologist who proposed this theory of needs in 1943 in a paper called 'A Theory of Human Motivation'. He believed that human beings have five needs that they share in common. The first four he termed 'deficiency' needs and the final one he defined as a 'need for self-actualisation'.

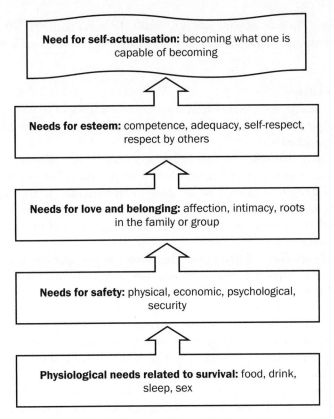

Based on Abraham Maslow's 'A Theory of Human Motivation'.

Maslow argued that all four deficiency needs (the bottom four needs in the diagram) have to be satisfied before people can achieve their potential – i.e. become self-actualised.

These needs relate to the overall human condition. However, they can be translated into those things we, as managers, can do to help create the space for people to motivate themselves in the workplace.

Physiological needs related to survival
For me, physiological needs are about having basic resources: a decent desk and chair; a living wage; a job description; a photocopier that works; breaks for coffee and tea; somewhere to make coffee and tea; access to information to help get the job done; a set of clearly laid-down policies and procedures; knowing when my appraisal is, when my one-to-ones are and who my boss is; and so on.

These might sound trivial, but I'm sure you will have had the experience of how disruptive people can be about what sometimes seems like the small stuff. When people's chairs are wobbly or the kettle breaks, it will affect their performance. So part of your job is to sweat the small stuff. Pay attention to people's basic ergonomic and physical needs and meet them to the best of your ability.

Needs for safety
A need for safety can be translated into a need for a sense of security and trust. When people are constantly afraid for their jobs, it makes it very difficult for them to concentrate.

You'd think that when human beings feel under threat of losing their jobs (either from redundancy or because they think you don't like or value them), the logical thing to do would be for them to work harder. In my experience, that rarely happens. Instead, most people start to worry and spend a great deal of time talking to their colleagues about their concerns, and that affects their performance.

Generally speaking, if you notice that someone isn't performing well, you can make sure that the person knows they aren't performing well, try to establish the underlying reasons for the poor performance, set clear targets and standards for them to meet within a specified timetable and, importantly, ensure that they have help and support to meet those standards.

However, if someone is normally a good worker but isn't performing well, it's a fair bet that it's as a result of feeling under threat and you will need to approach the issue a bit differently. You can't let standards drop, so you will still need to have the conversation about the employee's performance, as normal. However, in these circumstances, you will need to spend more time listening to their worries and make time to reassure them. You could do this by helping them understand the full financial picture of the organisation, how their department is performing, what actions are planned and so on. If there are financial issues in the organisation that mean there may be redundancies, you need to be honest about that and talk about what actions the organisation is taking to avoid having to make people redundant. If the individual really is under genuine threat, you should discuss what actions you will take to support them during any redundancy process.

Needs for love and belonging
This is about people's need to feel that they belong and that they are valued. Your job is to ensure that they feel they are part of the team, that their work is important and contributes to the overall goals of the team, and that they, as individuals, are valued and trusted.

This means giving plenty of praise and recognition – both privately and in public. Years ago, I worked for a chap called Ian Lawson who used to handwrite a thank-you card if you had done something particularly well and then post it to your home address. It felt so good to be able to open, in front of your family, something from your boss saying nice things about you and your work. People are desperate for positive reinforcement and they respond so well to it when they get it. My grandmother used to say 'you catch more flies with honey than with vinegar', and I have found that to be very true.

Praise without being meaningful isn't useful, however. You need to use the **five Rs**:

1. **Real:** Praise has to be genuine. People have inbuilt bullshit detectors – they'll know you're telling porkies if you praise them for something they didn't do that well. So make sure you're telling the truth. You can always find something genuine to praise.

2. **Relevant:** Praise must be specific to the particular work. General phrases such as 'you're working really hard' or 'that was a good piece of work' don't carry the same impact as 'that report you wrote was very good – it was punchy, with good examples and structured in such a way that it was easy to understand'.

3. **Regular:** I don't believe that you can overpraise people if the praise is genuine. In fact, we don't commend people anywhere near often enough, in my view. I don't know one person who says that they get too much praise. What do I say to that old mantra 'be sparing with your praise'? Pah! Make sure you are actively seeking opportunities to recognise people.

4. **Repeated:** Tell others about the praise you have just given to someone. Somehow, when someone says to me that they were talking to my chair and she said how effective I am at my job, it carries more weight than her telling me herself. Of course, you must tell the person directly, but make sure you repeat the praise to others too. For example, if you are sending an email to a member of your team thanking them for something, why not copy in your boss or the board of trustees?

5. **Robust:** Don't use wishy-washy language. Saying 'that's a nice pair of shoes' simply doesn't carry the same weight as 'daaaarling – what fabulous stilettos!' All joking aside, use big, strong words to emphasise the praise.

Needs for esteem

Money does not motivate people – or, at least, it certainly won't in the long term. A pay rise can give someone a brief high, but it doesn't last. And, indeed, it isn't really the money that motivates people but the recognition that accompanies it. I can point you to study after study and research paper after research paper that demonstrate this point. When people have decided to leave your organisation, however, they will nearly always look for a job with a higher salary – that makes sense, of course. Indeed, for the most part, it's safe to assume that they will tell you that the reason for their leaving is the need for more money. But, in my experience, salary is rarely the true motivator for the decision. The real question is, was it truly the money that made them start looking in the first place or was some other factor at play?

Of course, people do often look to leave because they feel genuinely ready to move on and because the best opportunities for them are outside the organisation. That's not a bad thing – it's more likely a reflection of how well you've developed them, and in such cases they will usually leave on good terms. However, sometimes folk leave for less positive reasons. They either feel they have nothing more to learn because they're not being developed or they don't feel that what they are doing is appreciated. People need to feel that they are good at their job, that they are making a valuable contribution to the work of the organisation and that their contribution is valued. This means you need to make sure that the work is interesting and varied, that they have freedom to make their own decisions in their work and that they have access to support if things go wrong. They need the reports they write to be read and acted on – not shoved in a drawer. They need to make their own presentations about their work – not have you do it for them. They need to attend board meetings so that they can listen to what the board says about their area and so they can answer questions directly themselves. And so on.

Need for self-actualisation

Self-actualisation is about the need for people to feel that they are being the kind of person they want to be and doing the kind of work they want to do. This concept is linked to a person's greater image of themselves, their values and their hopes and dreams. To help people fulfil this need, you should ask them about their aspirations and see what you can do to help them achieve those ambitions. For example, if you manage an accounts assistant who dreams of being a fundraiser, can you arrange for them to spend some time with the fundraising team? The most you can probably do is to create the space for people to help themselves.

There are limits, of course: you won't be able to send your accounts clerk off on shoe-making courses just because they want to be the next Manolo Blahnik!

McGregor's Theory X and Theory Y

In 1960, Douglas McGregor wrote a book called *The Human Side of Enterprise*, which built on Maslow's work. His basic premise was that assumptions made by managers about how people behave have a profound influence on how they actually behave. He believed that the type of behaviour exhibited in an individual is less to do with the personality of the individual than it is to do with the attitude and assumptions of the manager about that individual.

McGregor developed Theory X and Theory Y, which are two polarised summaries of how managers may view the people they are working with. Theory X managers assume that people dislike work and need to be directed and controlled in order to produce results. Theory Y managers believe that people are predisposed to like work and, under the right conditions, will seek to take responsibility for it.

The following table is my summary of the key points in each theory.

Theory X	Theory Y
People dislike work and will avoid it if they can	Work is necessary to people's psychological growth
People must be forced or bribed to make the right effort	People want to be interested in their work and, under the right conditions, they can enjoy it
People have to be told what to do	People will direct themselves towards a target that they understand and see as worthwhile
People would rather be directed than accept responsibilities	People will seek and accept responsibility under the right conditions
People are not self-disciplined	The discipline people impose on themselves is more effective and can be more severe than any imposed on them
People are motivated mainly by money	People are motivated mainly by the satisfaction of doing a good job
People are motivated by anxiety about their security	Under the right conditions, people are motivated by the desire to realise their own potential
Most people have little creativity except for when it comes to getting around management rules	Creativity and ingenuity are widely distributed and grossly underused

McGregor recognised that few managers hold either of these polarised extremes of beliefs about others. Nonetheless, if a person's beliefs about others' natural tendencies are biased one way or the other, either negatively or positively, they will affect how the person behaves – this equally applies to managers and the people they manage.

For example, if you believe that people are essentially lazy and need to be told what to do all the time, you are highly likely to find you have to spend a great deal of your time telling people what to do. On the other hand, if you believe that if you set the overall goal and give people the freedom to get on and achieve it, they will naturally go ahead and do so; you are more likely to find people putting in the extra effort.

I have found this to be very true in my own experience. Many years ago, I was given a promotion and, alongside the promotion, I was assigned a PA. Unbeknown to me, the previous manager had believed that this PA was not very good; I was given her because I was new and junior and hadn't yet proved that I deserved anyone of a higher calibre. (Plus, to be honest, my new line manager was not at all happy about having me in his team and I think was setting me up to fail – although, to give him the benefit of the doubt, he probably wasn't doing it deliberately.) In any event, no one told me that she was rubbish. I was young and naive, and I believed that I was getting someone really, really good. As a result, that was my assumption about her and so that's how I treated her: with a mixture of respect and awe! Of course, my assumption was spot on – she *was* brilliant. In fact, so brilliant that soon my colleagues were trying to nick her off me. What was the difference? Only that I genuinely believed I was getting the best, so that's how I behaved towards her. Accordingly, she stepped up and became the best. No effort was required on either side.

The lesson is that if you believe people are creative, intelligent, committed and competent, and that they want to grow and learn, then most of the time that is what you are likely to get.

Creating the right environment for your team

The main purpose of your job is to create the right environment so that your team can flourish. How do you do that? The answer is through resources, communication, opportunities and recognition.

Resources

In many not-for-profit organisations, it is a challenge to get adequate resources. We are always having to make a choice between something that we need for our beneficiaries and something that our staff members need in order to serve our beneficiaries, and those choices are not always straightforward. So, if you can afford decent resources (computers, tablets, smartphones, desks, chairs and so on), then cough up for them. And, if you can't, be open and honest about what the organisation has spent the money on instead so that the members of your team can see a clear reason why they're still having to put up with a wobbly chair and an ancient computer that crashes every hour!

Ask yourself:

- Do your team members have all the resources they need to do their job?
- Are the resources up to the required standard?
- If not, why not? Have you explained to your team why this is the case? Have you tried to get better stuff and does your team know that you've tried?

- If the resources aren't adequate but the job needs to be done anyway, what have you done to inspire and energise the members of your team so that they don't get stuck in Whingeville?
- How are the members of your team seated? Are they in the most efficient positions for communicating with each other and with people in other key departments?

It's very tempting to blame higher management for a lack of adequate resources. And it may well be that they've made really bad choices. As a member of the management team yourself, however, you can't join in with public moans about those choices. By all means, make your representations to the senior team about the resources your team needs, but never forget that there are always conflicting needs in any organisation. Resources are always tight and there will always be someone who doesn't get what they need – nine times out of ten for a good reason. If you don't know the reason, then find out and tell your team. But avoid falling into the trap of thinking that your team is being deliberately overlooked. It probably isn't. It's more likely that higher management believe that resources are more urgently needed elsewhere.

Communication
People like to know what's going on – and so they should. After all, it's largely down to their effort whether or not your organisation achieves its objectives, so people have every right to know whether or not their efforts are paying off. This means that you must prioritise communication.

Ask yourself:
- Do you have regular one-to-ones with team members?
- Do those one-to-ones last a minimum of half an hour?
- Are the one-to-ones focused on allowing team members to talk about how they believe they're doing?
- Does everyone understand the objectives of the department and their own job?
- Does everyone understand how their role fits into the wider team and organisation? Do they understand how they contribute to the ultimate organisational objectives?
- Do they know how they are performing, both as individuals and as a team?
- Do they have opportunities to raise issues and share ideas about how things could be done better or differently?

Opportunities
Most folk like to feel that their manager sees potential in them and that they are going to be given opportunities to grow and develop, both within the organisation and in terms of their own skill set. Even in small organisations, there are usually opportunities for growth and development. In fact, in my experience, it's almost easier to grow folk in smaller organisations than in larger ones, as there are lots of things to be done and fewer people to do them.

This means that many staff members end up doing work outside their own specific remit – and that is fantastic for personal development, career development, confidence and job satisfaction.

Ask yourself:

- Does everyone have a clear set of standards to achieve?
- Does everyone have, in addition to the minimum standards, targets for improvement?
- Are you delegating interesting work?
- Are you providing on- and off-the-job training?
- Do you allow team members who have expertise in an area to share that expertise with others?
- Do you structure roles so that people get to spend most of their time doing work that they enjoy and are good at?
- Do you encourage your team members to volunteer for other projects within the organisation?

Recognition

Rewards for achievement do not have to be monetary. In fact, in most not-for-profit organisations it is actually quite difficult to give people extra money to recognise their work. This is either because all the money is committed or because it isn't part of the culture. In any case, I don't think that people necessarily need money to feel recognised. Of course, no one is likely to turn down financial compensation, but the impact of it is very short lived. Moreover, it is likely to cause upset if someone finds out another person got more than they did!

The simplest sorts of reward send people home feeling important and valued – and, most of the time, they are not about money.

Ask yourself:

- Do you tell individuals face to face when they have done a good job?
- Do you publicly praise them to the senior managers and to the rest of the team?
- Do you ever send a written note or card to a person's home highlighting their achievement and thanking them for it?
- Do you take members of your team out for a drink or lunch when they've done a great job?
- Do you buy cakes to celebrate individual or team achievements?
- Do you occasionally reward individuals with extra time off that's not part of their holiday allowance?
- Do you give them extra authority and/or responsibility to recognise their abilities?
- Do you give or recommend promotions?

Offering basic support and supervision: one-to-ones

I talked earlier about one-to-ones (see 'Learning about your team' on page 21). They are so important because it's during your one-to-ones that you have the most focused opportunity to find out how motivated folk are and what they need from you in order to perform at their highest level.

It's too easy to cut one-to-ones short, cancel them or focus on simply giving out a list of jobs to be done rather than concentrating on overall performance.

Holding effective one-to-ones

An effective one-to-one will have the following key characteristics:

- It is a private meeting between the line manager and the staff member.
- The discussion is about the role as a whole, not just elements of it.
- It has an informal feel to it (which is why I recommend one-to-ones being held off-site over a cuppa) but, nonetheless, it has some structure so that it doesn't just feel like a regular chat.
- You allow time for the individual to talk through their general levels of motivation, job satisfaction and commitment.
- If they need to talk about something personal in their lives, you give them the space to do that.
- It covers the period between the last one-to-one and the current meeting, work in progress and the future.
- You keep notes of the actions that you have agreed.
- It is a two-way conversation, which means that you talk not only about the performance of the individual but also about your performance as a manager in supporting them. What more could you do? What are you doing less well? What do they need you to do more of?

During the one-to-one, your job is largely to ask questions. Below are some suggestions – not in any particular order – to prompt discussion. You will have others, of course.

- How do you feel the job has been going since our last one-to-one?
- What do you feel has gone well?
- What do you feel you do best?
- What do you feel you could have improved on?
- What problems have you encountered? How did you deal with them?
- What have you enjoyed most since the last one-to-one?
- What have you enjoyed least?
- In what ways could your job be improved?
- How are you getting on with other members of the team?
- How are you getting on with other members of the organisation?
- What extra support or training do you need?
- What can I do to help you?
- How could I be a better manager for you?

What you should never do at one-to-ones

You should never use a one-to-one to tell someone off or discipline them. If there is a performance issue, then, at the time the matter arises, arrange a special meeting to discuss it. The reason for this is that you want your team members to feel confident in their one-to-ones so that they are honest and open about how they are getting on. If they are afraid of getting into trouble or being on the receiving end of a negative reaction from you, then they are less likely to open up. If they don't open up, then you lose the opportunity to learn how to get the best out of them.

At DSC we talk about making your one-to-ones with your team members 'SUPER':

		Meaning	*Actions*

S		**Structured**	▪ Plan in advance what you intend to cover during the one-to-one
			▪ Keep notes as you go along during the month so you don't forget items you want to cover
			▪ Start with 'How are you?' – a general question to get a sense of their levels of motivation and commitment
			▪ Then ask the team member:
			  – What has gone/is going well and why?
			  – What is going less well and why?
			  – What support do they need from you?
			▪ End by agreeing targets for the coming month

U		**Usual**	▪ Make sure the meetings are planned a year in advance ▪ Make sure every team member has them in their diary ▪ **Golden rule number 1:** thou shalt always prioritise one-to-ones ▪ **Golden rule number 2:** thou shalt never cancel a one-to-one ▪ **Golden rule number 3:** if thou hast to break rule number 2, then rearrange the one-to-one for as close to the original date as possible
P		**Productive**	▪ Do your prep work before – don't just turn up ▪ Focus on what can be done, not what has gone wrong or what can't be done ▪ Think through some questions in advance to get the most out of the meeting

E	Exchanges	■ Let the team member do most of the talking – you should listen for 80% of the time ■ Your role is to ask questions and establish how the team member sees things ■ Always ensure that the team member knows you are there to support them whenever they need you
R	Recorded	■ Make brief notes about what you both talked about ■ Bring the notes with you to the next one-to-one so you can refer back to what you agreed and/or note where things have got better (or worse!)

Finally, it is inevitable that you will have to give negative feedback to a team member at some point. This is terribly hard to do, of course, but there are some simple steps you can take which will make it easier for you to give the feedback and easier for the individual to receive it and act on it. These are outlined in the following section.

Managing performance

Most large organisations have a formal performance management or appraisal system. Even if your organisation doesn't have one, it is important that you have a formal conversation at least once a year with each of your team members to discuss how well they have done, what they can do better, what support they need and what you are expecting of them in the coming year.

Whatever your system is, I am a firm believer in encouraging 360-degree feedback. This type of feedback involves an individual gathering input from a range of sources, including doing a self-evaluation and seeking feedback from managers, colleagues and any people whom they manage. Where relevant, they may also seek input from external stakeholders, such as customers or beneficiaries. 360-degree feedback is an incredibly useful mechanism for helping an employee to reflect on how their performance and behaviours at work make an impact on others – at all levels of the organisation. However, the process needs to be managed very carefully and all of the feedback given, both positive and negative, needs to be taken with a large pinch of salt and a hefty sense of perspective. In order to get the best out of this process, it is important to follow some simple rules.

Don't make the feedback anonymous or confidential

Anonymous feedback of any description is largely pointless. The whole point about feedback is that the individual should be able to act on it. If the employee doesn't know who said what, then they can't reasonably be expected to improve their behaviour.

Some time ago, I was coaching a CEO. At a meeting that I was observing, the chair told the CEO that 'some' people had 'some' problems with him. When I asked who had what problems, the chair said that she couldn't tell me or the CEO because she had been 'told in confidence'. I pointed out that if the CEO didn't know who had what problem, he could not reasonably be expected to make a judgement about what, if anything, needed to change. Therefore, his best course of action was simply to ignore the feedback. All the anonymous feedback achieved was to make the CEO feel undermined and lacking in confidence, and it left him absolutely no chance of doing anything about it. That's the problem with anonymity. You will remember from an earlier chapter me talking about how different people respond to different types of leadership (see 'What's your leadership style?' on page 34); well, the same is true for responding to others' behaviour. Someone may have given 360-degree feedback on one of your team members that says, for example, they think she or he talks too much in meetings. But, for all you know, there may well be another person in the team who really values those contributions. So, if you tell the team member to stop talking so much, then you may actually be disadvantaging someone else who finds it useful.

It's also important to note that context is everything. If your line manager has just told you off for poor time-keeping or has held you to account for your performance, you are much more likely to say something negative about them. Or, if you don't get on well with a fellow member of your team, you are more likely to blame them than yourself. The messenger matters.

It is important to create an atmosphere of openness and honesty. Encouraging folk to own their feedback about their colleagues and bosses is much more likely to give you a reasonable assessment of how individuals are seen by others than if you allow feedback to remain anonymous. The trick is how you frame the questions and how you interpret the answers.

Use simple questions to get the right sort of feedback

I recommend three core questions, plus a supplementary one if it is a manager who is being appraised:

1. What has X done well?
2. What could X have done differently?
3. What should X's priorities be for the coming year?
4. For managers: What works in X's leadership style and what could X consider changing?

These questions broadly cover the sort of information you are trying to gather. Most decent folk will naturally be reluctant to stick the boot in on question 2. That is why question 3 is the key one because it is in what people say about priorities that you get a more honest assessment of what the individual has done well or less well.

Your job as the manager is to put it all in perspective. Don't take at face value any individual feedback. Look for common themes; if there is an outlier, there's a good chance that that feedback is more about the individual giving it than the person receiving it. Discuss with the employee what their interpretation of the feedback is. Where is it justified and where is it not? If an individual said the employee was either 'awesome' or 'awful', why? What might have been going on at the time to lead to such an appraisal? Context is everything!

Discuss and interpret the feedback

- Ask the employee for their thoughts and views on the feedback. Does it reflect what they think? Was there anything unexpected and, if so, what and why?
- Ask the employee whether there is anything they feel they need to change as a result of the feedback.
- Ask the employee whether there is anything they need from you as a line manager to support them.
- Focus on actions for the future: are there relationships that aren't working well? What can the employee do about them?
- Make it clear that you are on their side. Your role in the feedback process is that of a coach and a supporter.

Make sure you've managed the process well

As the line manager, it is your job to make sure that the conversation about the 360-degree feedback goes well. If the employee leaves the meeting feeling undermined and unconfident, you have not managed the process well. You will know you have done a good job if the employee:

- leaves the meeting feeling empowered and appreciated;
- has a healthy sense of what they do well and less well;

- has reasonable plans if change is needed;
- knows that you have their back and intend to support them in whatever way they need.

Managing staff is hard work – there is no doubt about that. But get it right and you will have a happy and productive team (most of the time, anyway!) who do great work to support your organisation's aims. What could be more rewarding than that?

Remember

1. People want to do well at work – your job is to create the space for them to shine.
2. You catch more flies with honey than with vinegar.
3. Have proper, planned and diarised one-to-ones where you let your team members do most of the talking.
4. Context is everything!

5 Building your team

If I could solve all the problems myself, I would.

A reply attributed to Thomas Edison when asked why he had a team of 21 assistants

There are many elements that go into making a team either effective or ineffective: from the characters, skills and personalities of the individuals to the distribution of responsibilities to how the team makes decisions. As a manager, you need to be able to manage all of these elements because, in order to get the job done, you need people who are able to work together in unison.

Most likely you have inherited the people who are currently in your team. However, there may be times when you get the opportunity to choose a new team member yourself.

Choosing the right person for the team

You can find numerous books about good recruitment practices and selection of staff, so I'm not going to cover the legalities and basic processes in this book. What I am going to focus on is how you make your choices and look at the more human side of choosing a new team member.

When a team member leaves, I strongly advise you to take some time first to review the job they were doing, consider how it fits into the team as a whole and evaluate the overall skills of the team.

Many of us make the mistake of only thinking about the individual job that needs to be done, but it is just as important to look at how that job fits into the overall purpose of the team. Ask yourself the following questions:

- Is this job still needed?
- Has anything changed since the position was created?
- Is the job serving the right function for the right team?
- Are there elements of the job that could (or should) be done by someone else?
- What skills does the team lack overall?
- Can the job be amended to incorporate those skills that are currently missing from the team?

I suggest involving the team in these discussions. You may learn some things about tasks and other aspects of your staff members' work that you didn't know, and having them involved will make it easier for you if you want to make some key changes.

Once you are sure that the job is still needed and fits in with the team's objectives, you have to consider the type of person you are looking for. This is an interesting one. There's often a dilemma between choosing the person who is best qualified for the job and the person who will fit best into the team. And there is no hard or fast answer to this one. The fact is that if you have a member of the team who doesn't fit, it can affect the overall performance of the team. On the other hand, choosing someone who is going to be popular in the team might mean that you don't get the quality of delivery in the job that you need. Plus, it may well be useful for your team to have a bit of a shake-up.

Of course, you need team unity to a certain degree; however, life is not as simple as that. Ultimately, you need to remember that your objective is to ensure the team is performing well and not necessarily worry about whether everyone is hanging out together at weekends because they like each other so much.

I once led a team where one of the team members was not perceived to be a team player at all, and that caused huge resentment in the rest of the team. In our one-to-ones, the other members of the team were constantly complaining about this team member. But the reality was that she outperformed them by an enormous amount. Each of them had yearly targets to generate £60,000 and she brought in around £150,000 – year after year. I knew that if I changed that individual, the whole performance of the department would plummet. So, in that instance, I decided that the overall objectives of the department were more important than the fact that the team did not operate as one. Of course, I did all the usual stuff of trying to help her to integrate more and getting the rest of the team to understand the value she brought in terms of our aim of achieving the overall objectives of the organisation. None of it worked – or at least not sustainably. But, from the perspective of achieving our outcomes, the fact is that we had three really successful years until she left. Then – surprise, surprise – our overall performance went back to good, rather than outstanding. What I have never forgotten is that despite the tedious (for me, anyway!) conflict within the team, the overall performance of the rest of the team went up as a result of her being with us and down when she left. Sometimes, you just have to tell people to get over themselves and think about the greater needs of the organisation. And sometimes, as a manager, you just have to absorb the whinges and carry on doing what you think is right.

When it comes to a choice between attitude and experience, personally, I usually go for the right attitude. You can always give someone experience, but it is hugely difficult to get people to change their attitudes. Someone with the right attitude will work hard to gain the experience they need, and you can teach them any skills they are lacking. When I say 'attitude', I don't mean that they will prioritise getting on with the rest of the team; I mean that they will be willing and open, and prepared to knuckle down and get on with it.

The manager's role in the team

Time and time again, I have seen managers lose sight of their role in the team. You are *not* part of the team you lead – you are the leader of the team. The team to which you *belong* is the rest of the management team. You need to retain a certain degree of critical distance from the team you manage in order to make the right decisions and monitor performance effectively. If you get too close to your team, it makes it much harder to take the sometimes tough decisions about individuals that you need to take.

Equally, it is not your job to represent your team to more senior management – it is your job to represent senior management to your team. This means that you need to hold the management line. You must never knock management decisions to your team, no matter how frustrated you are about decisions that have been taken. There are several common-sense reasons for this. Firstly, if you knock management, you are subliminally knocking yourself, as you are part of management and they have made the decision to appoint you. Secondly, you are paid as a manager, so it is neither appropriate nor professional to diss the management of the organisation to those junior to you. Thirdly, it is destabilising for the team and, furthermore, it makes it harder for you to be credible. Think about it: if your team members believe you have no influence over or don't respect senior management, then why on earth should they believe in and respect you?

If you don't like something, fight about it behind closed doors with your management colleagues or your own boss. Once the decision has been made, however, you must see it through positively. (Of course, I don't include whistleblowing for serious misconduct in this.) If holding the agreed management line is something you simply can't live with, well then ... honestly? You need to move on and find another job. You wouldn't want people in your team to be disloyal to you, would you? Your management colleagues won't want you to be disloyal to them either.

61

How well is your team working together?

It is helpful to have a baseline to measure how well your team is working together. Below is a questionnaire I designed to help you establish that. You don't have to use the statements I have put – you can, of course, create your own.

The way to use the questionnaire is to get team members to complete it at a team meeting. Then go round and ask people what their scores are for each individual question. If you find that everyone is broadly in agreement and the overall team score for a statement is fairly high, then you probably don't need to spend time discussing it. If, however, the overall team score for a statement is low, then you might want to talk about why the score is low and what the team can do about it. Similarly, if there is a wide discrepancy between the scores for a statement, you should address that with the team.

The useful thing about an exercise like this is that it is a way of helping individuals within the team to vocalise problems they perceive without personalising them. And it helps you, as the manager, to see where problem areas lie and identify potential solutions for them.

Team self-assessment: how well do the following statements describe your team?

For each statement, choose a score from 1 (strongly disagree) to 10 (strongly agree).

The team:

1 Has a common understanding of the organisation's vision, mission and purpose

Low				Medium					High
1	2	3	4	5	6	7	8	9	10

2 Sees itself as accountable for the overall performance of the department and organisation

Low				Medium					High
1	2	3	4	5	6	7	8	9	10

3 Constantly seeks to improve the organisation/department

Low				Medium					High
1	2	3	4	5	6	7	8	9	10

4 Focuses on solutions not problems

Low				Medium					High
1	2	3	4	5	6	7	8	9	10

5   Engages in robust and useful debate

Low   Medium   High

1	2	3	4	5	6	7	8	9	10

6   Focuses on clients, service users and beneficiaries (as appropriate)

Low   Medium   High

1	2	3	4	5	6	7	8	9	10

7   Publicly shows a united front

Low   Medium   High

1	2	3	4	5	6	7	8	9	10

8   Has a high level of empathy and co-operation with one another

Low   Medium   High

1	2	3	4	5	6	7	8	9	10

9   Communicates openly, honestly and appropriately with one another

Low   Medium   High

1	2	3	4	5	6	7	8	9	10

10   Demonstrates trust and loyalty to one another

Low   Medium   High

1	2	3	4	5	6	7	8	9	10

Use the questionnaire as an opportunity to have a conversation about what kinds of behaviour you want from the team and how they can work together most effectively.

Understanding team dynamics

Here comes the science bit! There are some interesting theories about what happens when groups of people get together, and I think it's worth having some awareness of the research around this subject. I'm going to explain some of the theoretical approaches to group dynamics, but not in any detail – I will simply provide enough information to get you thinking about how you might usefully apply this information when developing your own team. If you are interested in exploring these issues in more detail, some relevant books are listed in the recommended reading list (see page 128).

Creation of group norms

Muzafer Sherif did an experiment in the early part of the twentieth century examining how group norms were created. In simple terms, he set up an experiment that asked individuals to determine whether a pinpoint of light moved or not. He discovered that individuals' judgements about this varied widely. However, if these same individuals were put in a group with others who spoke their judgement loudly and confidently, they subsequently adapted their original view to fit in with the view of those others. Even when individuals were then separated from the loud, confident others, they persisted in their adapted view.

Another experiment, by Solomon Asch in the 1950s, also examined this issue of group pressure towards conformity. In Asch's experiment, there was a set of participants and a number of what is termed 'confederates' (in psychological experiments these are individuals who, unknown to the participants, are in cahoots with the experimenter) who had agreed what their answer would be before starting the experiment. The participants were asked to determine which of the lines on the right of the illustration below were longer than the line on the left, or the same length, and so on – in all cases, the answer was obvious. Individuals had to announce their responses publicly and the confederates always got their response in first.

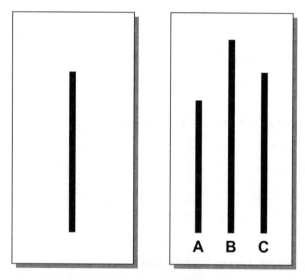

The two diagrams used in Solomon Asch's experiment.

What Asch found was that the participants amended their view to fit in with the views of the confederates almost 40% of the time, even if the confederates were clearly wrong. This can be compared with the control group (i.e. the group in which there were no confederates) where, given this lack of outside influence, only 1 in 35 people gave an incorrect answer.

This experiment on line lengths showed that pressure to conform varies between individuals – some people will manage to remain independent despite the circumstances. Nonetheless, the pressure to amend an individual view to fit in with others – especially if those others are seen as stronger, more opinionated, more knowledgeable, and so on – is very strong. This is particularly a problem at work, where the right or wrong answer is not always as obvious as it is in Asch's line experiment.

This is why majority voting can be dangerous. Even though some people will be confident about stating their opinion regardless of the situation, if you create an environment where disagreement is not encouraged, you make it harder for people to go against others' views, especially if it is the majority they are disagreeing with. Therefore, create an environment where dissent is open and discussed and not punished in the group. A simple trick is to go round the group and ask for everyone's views on a particular topic. Don't just rely on folk to speak out, because that encourages the less confident to hide behind the others and it means that you won't hear information or opinions that might be incredibly useful.

Similarly, if people are appearing to be a bit wishy-washy, then ask them to rate their response to the suggestion or matter under discussion. For example, 'George has suggested that we move the staff briefing day to a Monday. On a scale of 1 to 10, how much do you agree?' People who disagree with the majority but aren't comfortable voicing their opinion out loud, meaning that their dissent would otherwise go unnoticed, will find it almost impossible to say out loud a number that is incongruent with how they really feel. It's the strangest thing and I'm not sure why it happens, but the fact that it does makes it really useful! This is because if somebody says 5 or 7, you can ask what it would take for them to say 10, or why they can't say 10 now. This is likely to open up real discussion and therefore mitigate against the danger of groupthink.

Polarisation of group views

Polarisation of group views describes the situation where the final decision of a group is more extreme than the aggregate of the group members' views. Essentially, in these cases, the number of arguments for or against a particular argument carries more weight than the actual strength of the arguments. Here's an example of how this might work: let's say a team is debating whether to adopt a more or less risky approach to a problem. After an initial discussion, a few people voice a weak preference for the riskier option. As the discussion continues, more arguments are put forward that agree with the previously voiced arguments, but without any of these new arguments being any stronger. In this way, the group gradually becomes more strongly in favour of risk-taking, but simply as a result of momentum. No convincing argument has been put forward and there has been no real examination of the alternative option.

Margaret Wetherell, a prominent psychologist, did a series of experiments in the 1980s which examined how much people's perceptions of others in a group affected how they made decisions and what positions they were most likely to support. She looked at what are termed 'in-groups' and 'out-groups' – that is, those groups that are perceived as either similar or dissimilar to the individual concerned. She discovered that people will tend to side first with an in-group which they perceive as similar to themselves, secondly with an in-group which is dissimilar to themselves, thirdly with an out-group which is similar to themselves, and finally with an out-group which is dissimilar to themselves. See the diagram below.

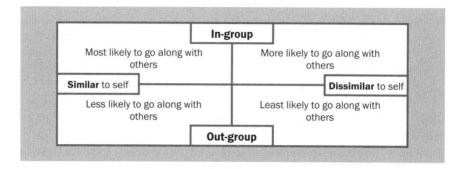

Wetherell also discovered that people have a tendency to consider the source of a piece of information as relevant as the information itself. In other words, the 'messenger' makes a big difference to how a message is heard. Furthermore, group members have a tendency to conform to an exaggerated stereotype of their group position.

So, as the manager, your job is to minimise the divisions between people by helping them to focus on the similarities between them rather than the differences. To ensure that individuals' perceptions of others don't cloud their decision-making, it helps to ask people to rationalise the position they are taking in reference to the facts and evidence at hand – this will make them consider the situation more than the messenger. As a result, the group members are more likely to hear and debate a broad spectrum of input and, therefore, are more likely to make richer and more effective decisions.

Decision-making in groups

This whole business of decision-making in groups is an interesting one. During the Second World War, the government wanted housewives to change their families' dietary habits to eat less popular cuts of meat. A psychologist called Kurt Lewin conducted an experiment where he gathered together two groups of housewives. One group received a lecture by an expert about using cuts of meat. The other group learned the facts from an expert but were then allowed to discuss the information they had received together. In the first group, only 3% of the women subsequently changed their habits and served the less popular cuts of meat. In the second group, however, a different picture emerged with 32% of women serving the more unpopular cuts.

For me this clearly suggests that this happened for two main reasons. Firstly, during discussions, a new group norm emerges which is apparent to the participants and, therefore, makes it more likely that they will conform with that norm. Secondly, when they are able to make their own decision, individuals are more likely to carry it out.

The above findings reinforce the importance of managers allowing teams to discuss problems and situations and work out for themselves how to solve them. Indeed, training programmes are often designed with that same end in mind. If the trainer simply tells the trainees what to do, they are much less likely to do it compared to when they discover the answer for themselves. So, don't be fooled. You might think it's quicker and more effective to just tell people the answer or what to do, but, actually, if you do that, you are much less likely to get the team to do what needs to be done. And no amount of authority will change that.

To get your team to *want* to do something, get them involved in deciding what needs to be done.

Group psychodynamics: projection

Broadly speaking, the psychoanalytical approach says that we are influenced by what happens to us as children – at different ages, according to different psychoanalytic approaches (those of Freud, Jung, Klein and so on). When we are children, there are things that we want and things that we don't want. We will actively work to get the things we want (sweets, toys, affection) and seek to avoid or defend ourselves against things we don't want (broccoli, chores, punishment). This means that we learn certain behaviours as a child that work well for us in the context of childhood, but we can unconsciously carry those same behaviours into adulthood, where they may be less effective.

For example, in the workplace, we may unconsciously adopt these defence mechanisms we developed in our childhood to help us avoid negative or difficult situations or to help us find a way to not feel bad about ourselves. A classic defence mechanism is 'projection', which is where we 'project' our own feelings onto others, thereby attributing those feelings to them. You will notice this in your team when someone comes to you and says 'people are unhappy', or something similar – beware of taking those comments at face value. Often, the self-appointed rep is actually projecting onto others how they themselves feel but aren't acknowledging. Always ask the individual how *they* feel and, if they say they're fine, then advise them to tell those folk who are unhappy to come and speak with you directly.

Projection, in group terms, can also result in the creation of 'heroes', 'villains' and 'scapegoats'. For example, the group may identify an individual within the team whom they consider to be the hero, and that person's view will tend to carry more weight than someone whom the group have decided is the villain. When it is difficult for members of a group to express themselves, one member may become 'the angry one' on behalf of the group and the rest of the group will hide behind them. Equally, if someone is perceived by the group as a 'star', then they are more likely to have their behaviours copied. Scapegoating can be seen when folk attribute failure to follow a process or rule (for example, missing a deadline, turning up late or producing a poor-quality report) to another person or group of people rather than acknowledging themselves to be at fault.

Projection can be either 'benign' or 'malign'. In benign projection, the team members are more likely to be open to having their perceptions about the group or individual in question challenged if they are exposed to facts and evidence. In malign projection, no such 'reality check' takes place and the individual or group being maligned cannot escape the label, regardless of how they really feel, or they adopt the position, action or behaviour they are being accused of. It is your job, as a manager, to make all the relevant facts and evidence apparent to your team members and ensure they evaluate them.

Building your perfect team

At this stage you have a better understanding of why teams behave in the way that they do from a psychological perspective. But how do you build this perspective into your day-to-day managing? This is where the brilliantly useful work of a chap called Bruce Tuckman comes into play. Back in the 1960s, he did a lot of research into the stages of group development, which he broke down as 'forming', 'storming', 'norming' and 'performing'. The table below summarises the key elements of each stage, how the leader and each of the team members fit in, and how to move teams from one part of the process to the next.

Tuckman's four stages of team development

I find this a really useful toolkit when I'm thinking about any stage of a team's development.

	Forming	Storming	Norming	Performing
Character-istics	■ Politeness ■ Tentative joining in ■ Unstable membership ■ Orienting personally and professionally ■ Gathering impressions ■ Avoiding controversy and conflict ■ Hidden agendas ■ Formation of cliques ■ Need for safety, acceptance and approval	■ Struggles over purpose and goals ■ Vying for leadership ■ Evidence of differences in points of view and personal style ■ Lack of role clarity ■ Reliance on voting, arbitration and leader-made decisions ■ Team organising itself and its work	■ Cohesion and harmony ■ Striving for balance ■ Open-mindedness ■ Building of trust ■ Comfortable relationships ■ Dissolution of cliques ■ Focus on and energy for tasks ■ Thinking about *how* the team functions ■ Confidence and creativity	■ Team being fully functional ■ Clear roles ■ Interdependent relationships ■ Team being able to organise itself ■ Flexibility ■ Members functioning well individually, in subgroups and as a whole team ■ High degree of empathy for one another
Team identity	■ Individual identities more important than the team's identity	■ Lessening of emphasis on individual identity ■ Building of team identity	■ Team identity begins to emerge clearly	■ Team identity is strong

	Visionary	Facilitator	Coach	Adviser
Leader's role	■ Provides structure and clear task direction ■ Allows time for people to get to know one another ■ Creates atmosphere of confidence and optimism ■ Is actively involved in the team	■ Acknowledges conflict ■ Guides towards consensus ■ Gets members to assume more task responsibility ■ Teaches conflict-resolution mechanisms ■ Offers support and praise ■ Is actively involved in the team	■ Gives feedback and support ■ Encourages resolution of conflict individually and as a team ■ Plans celebrations ■ Challenges thinking ■ Allows for less structure ■ Continues to focus on building strong relationships ■ Is less involved in the team	■ Gives positive reinforcement and support ■ Challenges thinking ■ Presents new challenges ■ Gives feedback ■ Encourages change and development
Team member's role	■ Asks questions to be clear about the team's task ■ Avoids cliques ■ Gets to know everyone ■ Is patient with the process ■ Listens ■ Suspends judgement	■ Considers all views ■ Initiates ideas ■ Works towards consensus ■ Is aware of others' needs ■ Accepts conflict as natural ■ Respects diversity of style, approach and views	■ Thinks about how they can influence how the team works together ■ Remains realistic ■ Doesn't purposefully avoid conflict ■ Is flexible ■ Supports efforts to build team spirit ■ Initiates and considers new ideas	■ Keeps overall goals in mind ■ Remains flexible ■ Maintains momentum ■ Offers new challenges, where appropriate ■ Provides information ■ Offers support ■ Is aware of and works with team values and norms
Ways to get stuck	■ Staying too polite ■ Lack of clear direction	■ Lack of conflict-resolution skills ■ Lack of a person to facilitate conflict resolution ■ Individuals getting stuck on their own agendas ■ Turf wars and tree-hugging (i.e. refusing to let go of favourite projects, processes or ways of working)	■ Groupthink ■ Too much comfort ■ Focus on relationships, ignoring tasks ■ Unwillingness to take risks ■ Avoidance of conflict	■ Burnout ■ Team not evaluating or monitoring itself

Bridge to the next stage	■ Adequate comfort level	■ Collective win	■ Confidence/ risk-taking	■ Reflection/ evaluation
Conflict	■ Low	■ High	■ Low	■ Healthy
Output	■ Low	■ Low	■ Low to medium	■ High

Based on Bruce Tuckman's classifications of the stages of group development.

Creating an effective team is an ongoing process and the development of it is always cyclical. As the team members change or develop, there will be a natural ebb and flow and you will find yourself moving from one team level to another. The trick is to be able to spot which stage your team is at and then take the appropriate actions to move them to where you need them to be.

Remember

1. It's not about who you've got in the team; it's about what you do with them.
2. Taking the time to understand the underlying psychology of a team will help you to manage it better.
3. Teams ebb and flow – notice what stage they're in and respond accordingly.

6 Getting the job done

Each morning sees some task begin,
Each evening sees it close;
Something attempted, something done,
Has earned a night's repose.
Henry Wadsworth Longfellow, 'The Village Blacksmith'

Getting the job done. Ultimately, this is what you're there for, right? The reality is that you can have highly developed individuals and a happy, fun-loving team, but, if you're not achieving the task, you're certainly not going to get any brownie points!

Here's the thing. We develop individuals and build teams in order to achieve the objective of our team and organisation. Although it's rewarding to do in and of itself, we are actually doing it for a purpose.

Achieving the task is very much about focusing on our practical management skills rather than our more ephemeral leadership skills, which I talked about earlier. This chapter takes the framework described in chapter 3 (see 'A simple toolbox' on page 29) and breaks down the heading 'task' into detailed steps that will help you achieve your tasks.

Key actions
As a reminder, you need to:
- define your objectives;
- plan;
- brief and communicate;
- monitor and support;
- evaluate.

And then start all over again!

Define objectives
This is *the* most important part of achieving the task. You need to be absolutely clear what the end result is – that is, what it is you are trying to achieve. Please note that I'm specifically talking about the *end* result here. One of the things my organisation does is provide training and publications to charities. And we do it well. But many years ago, when things weren't going as well as I hoped they would, it was obvious that we seemed to have lost a sense of direction and the ability to innovate. I came to realise that we had forgotten our purpose. We had begun to confuse *what* we did with *why* we existed and, as a result,

concentrated on what we were comfortable doing: providing publications and training programmes.

However, *what* we do is not *why* we do it. Our charitable object is to promote the efficiency and efficacy of charities. There are myriad ways of doing that, with the provision of publications and training being only two of them. By forgetting the overall objective of the organisation, we had forgotten to think about other ways in which we could achieve our objects. Once we had remembered what we were trying to achieve, suddenly, all sorts of other possibilities emerged which we had not really considered before, such as employment law clubs, online services, articles and newsletters.

It's not enough to simply know what it is you do – you need to know what you are trying to achieve by doing it, and what it will look like when you've done it.

Defining the objectives is not only about the wider organisation's vision; it's also about the purpose of any specific task. For example, you may have been asked to get your team to produce a report about your future funding prospects. The report is the task, but what is it that the task is supposed to achieve for you? Is it to persuade someone that you need more resources? Or to keep someone informed as to the activity you are planning? Or to reassure someone that you know what you're doing? Knowing what the report is meant to achieve will make a big difference to how you go about getting the job done. Therefore, before even embarking on designing the report, you need to establish:

- What is the report going to be used for? Will it help your organisation to make a decision about which potential funders to approach? Will it help you to agree on what costs to cut? And so on.
- Who is going to read it? Therefore, what language, style and examples will be most effective at providing your audience with the information they need and making sure you achieve your objective.

Once you are clear about the overall objective, you need to think about what sorts of activities you are going to need to undertake in order to get the task done. You also need to consider what sorts of things might get in the way of the task being done (for example, limited funds or no staff being available) and think of ways in which you might overcome these constraints or work around them. Planning things thoroughly is vital to ensure you don't get stuck on the route to achieving your end result.

Plan

Sun Tzu, who apparently lived in ancient China sometime between 770 and 476 BC, is the alleged author of *The Art of War*, a book which is widely used as a metaphor for leadership. He is purported to have said that 'the purpose of a plan is to calm the heart before the heat of battle'. In other words, having a plan gives you the confidence to act – the details of the plan are secondary. Although understanding how you aim to tackle the stages of your task is crucial, it is worth remembering that the details of your plan will almost never come to pass exactly as you envisage. Once you put a plan into action, things will inevitably change.

Another reason to keep in mind this fluid nature of plans is to avoid the danger of over-planning. Or, indeed, of spending so much time planning that we not only lose the battle but actually miss it altogether. In my experience, the most effective plans have:

- a broad overview of the tasks to be done;
- a basic breakdown of what needs to be done by when and by whom;
- some idea of the resources that are likely to be required.

A plan also needs to be something that people can broadly remember – they shouldn't have to turn to page 73, paragraph 5.10 of the three-year plan to remind themselves of what needs to be done. Further, if the plan has too much detail, you take away from folk the ability to decide how best to achieve what needs to be done. Even in the military, renowned for its planning, they have a concept called 'mission command'. This is where the leader of the team is told what the end objective is and what they need to deliver, but it is then up to them to decide how to get it done (obviously within the relevant parameters, such as budget, resources, etc.).

It is important to link the purpose of the plan to the overall objectives of the organisation. This helps to give context to what it is you are asking people to do and makes it more likely that the plan will succeed. For instance, let's imagine that your objective as an organisation is to prevent cruelty to children, your particular department is involved in managing the accounts and you are asked to implement a new accounting system. You could say that the purpose of the new system is to ensure that the accounts are produced quickly and accurately, so that others in the charity don't spend their precious time fiddling with figures and are instead better able to serve the children.

Planning, however, isn't always about huge projects. More often it's about planning the team's work for the week or the month. It doesn't really matter whether it's a huge task or a small one – the basic essentials of planning don't change. You need to gather information, consider the options, check resources, consult with the team and develop their ideas. Then you can decide on priorities, timescales, standards and targets, who is doing what job and so on. The planning stage might be as quick as ten minutes or as long as several days – it will all depend on the size of the task or project and the people involved.

Gather information

Before you decide what it is you are going to do, you need to find out what you need to know to make that decision – i.e. gather information. Again, this doesn't have to be a lengthy process, as most of the plans we make are for the immediate future, not for long-term strategy. However, that doesn't mean skimping on the process. You might, at your monthly or weekly team meeting, ask the members of your team what they have planned for the week, where they are at on certain projects or pieces of work, what they anticipate coming up during the week or month, and so on. This will give you some idea of what your resources are likely to be and how flexible your team members are. You can then consult the team and find out whether they have any ideas which can be developed and incorporated into the plan, to help you to deliver your objective.

I cannot stress enough how incredibly important it is to consult your team. Anybody asked to implement a plan that they have had no part in designing is likely to find flaws in it – on principle! And any normal human being is going to find it hard to be fully committed and motivated to implement something that has been forced on them – no matter how sensible the plan seems to you. Finally, when you involve people, if you do make a decision about how to proceed that is against what they believed, at least they can't turn around and say, 'Well, nobody asked me!'

Lots of managers worry about consulting because they are concerned about creating expectations that they might not be able to meet or that the team will think that the decision has to be a majority view. You may well be able to make some of your decisions by arriving at a consensus, but that's probably more of a bonus than a general rule of thumb. Often folk will disagree on the best course of action, which is why you, as the manager, have the responsibility to make the decision – and own it if it goes wrong.

The simplest thing to do, before you consult, is to make it absolutely clear that you are consulting to get a wide range of views which you will then consider before making your decision. Communicate that you will take into account people's suggestions but that, ultimately, your job as the manager is to make the decision you feel is best, based on the knowledge you have. It is not your job to please the team but to get the job done. Being honest about that is really helpful. Most folk respond to that sort of honesty with an adult understanding of your role in decision-making and are happy to be asked and to be given the opportunity to influence your decision.

You also need to consider what skill sets you have within the team that you can make use of – not only those that are already well developed (for example, someone who is great with service users or beneficiaries, or someone who is particularly skilled at Excel) but also those that you can develop further.

Decide

Once you've gathered all the information, consulted and had a bit of a think, you will be ready to make the decision. This is when the work really begins!

You need to decide on the priorities. Many people struggle with prioritising but, actually, it's fairly straightforward. You prioritise those tasks that are most likely to help you achieve the objectives. This means distinguishing between the 'must be done', the 'ought to be done' and the 'would be nice to get done'. For instance, in the finance team, banking the cheques must be done, otherwise you don't have the cash to pay the bills; doing the bank reconciliations ought to be done, otherwise you don't know exactly what invoice relates to what cheque; and analysing the ratio of cheques received to BACS payments made would be nice to get done, but can wait until you can create the time for it (unless the analysis is needed as input for some bigger strategic plan).

You also need to be clear about timescales, standards and accountability. Decide what needs to be done by when and to what standard, and who is going to be responsible for doing it. Again, this is where it's very easy to slip up. Don't say things like 'as soon as possible' or 'when you get the chance'. That's unclear and leaves people unsure of what to prioritise. Be specific: 'The week's cheques need to be banked by 5pm on Thursday.' But also, make sure you explain why the deadline matters and what the consequences of not meeting it are. So, 'The week's cheques need to be banked by 5pm on Thursday because if they're not done by then, the cheques don't clear in time for the salaries to be paid on Monday, and, therefore, we end up in overdraft ...' and so on.

If you're clear about the consequences, people are much more likely to meet the deadline. If they feel that it doesn't matter, then they'll prioritise something else which they think is more important or which they prefer doing.

Always being clear about your expectations for how a task should be done is helpful to everyone. I don't mean you should interfere in the detail, because that isn't effective delegation (which I'm going to go into much more detail about in the following section). I'm referring to making sure that your team members know what your expectation is about the 'final product', so to speak. For example, 'The report needs to be emailed to me by Friday 4pm; it should be no more than four sides of A4, summarising the fundraising plan with your recommendation as to which potential funder is the priority.' This level of detail gives enough information about what you're expecting while still giving the team member the freedom to decide how to do the job.

Basically, when it comes to decision-making, you need to consider the five Cs:

Consider	■ What is it that you are trying to achieve? ■ Whose decision is it? ■ What kind of decision is it? (Consensus? Unilateral?) ■ What do you need to know in order to make the decision? ■ Whom do you need to involve? ■ What is your timescale to a) make the decision and b) get the job done? ■ What are the ramifications of the decision? ■ Who will be affected by the decision?
Consult	■ Those people who have information that will help you to make the decision ■ Those people who will be affected by the decision you take ■ Those people whom you trust to test your thinking ■ Think about the most effective way of consulting; the more important the decision, the more consultation needs to be done face to face
Commit	■ Take time to think ■ Identify more than one option ■ Check facts that you are not sure of ■ Ask someone independent about your decision ■ Remind yourself of what you are trying to achieve ■ Ask yourself: am I making the right decision for the right reasons? ■ Consider the impact and consequences of any decision you make ■ If in doubt, make the decision that is going to help to achieve the organisation's purpose most effectively ■ Consider how you will implement the decision and who needs to be involved ■ Consider how, when and to whom to communicate the decision

Communicate	■ Communicate your decision to all those you have consulted, all those who are affected by the decision, and your senior colleagues ■ Communicate the 'why' as well as the 'what' ■ Remind people of the decision-making process you went through ■ The bigger the decision, the more important it is to communicate it face to face, with your message backed up in writing
Check	■ Did you make the right decision? ■ Is it working? ■ Was it communicated effectively, i.e. does everyone know what was decided and why? ■ Is everyone committed to delivering the decision? ■ Does anything need to be changed or amended? ■ Give and receive feedback on the process, the decision itself and the implementation of it ■ Praise those involved often and sincerely

Delegate

The ability to delegate effectively is very important – but so many managers get it terribly wrong! It's easy to confuse task *allocation* with *delegation* – they're not really the same thing.

Allocation is where you're only assigning a task. Essentially, you're asking a team member to carry out a job exactly as you would do it or as it has always been done – there is often no room for innovation and creativity. And, indeed, there are some tasks that are like that – where there is little opportunity to try doing things differently (sometimes, there is literally only one way to carry out a task!). But there are also a lot of tasks where allowing someone the freedom to decide how it is done is not just good for the individual's development but is also beneficial for the organisation.

Delegation is when you deliberately choose to give a member of your team the authority to carry out a piece of work that you would normally do yourself. It also implies committing power to that person to make the decisions, entrusting them to produce the final result, or sending or authorising a person as a representative. Lloyd and Rothwell, when describing the benefits of delegation, say that effective delegation ensures that:

■ Leaders are spending their time wisely on important issues that merit their attention.

- Staff are being developed and grown in their jobs by being given opportunities to learn new skills.
- Work is being carried out at the lowest safe level in the organisation and decisions are being made close to the real action thereby reducing costs and the likelihood of error.

How to delegate effectively

Every job can be broken down into three levels:

1. **Responsibility:** This is the 'doing' part of the job. In other words, if you are responsible for writing a report, you are the person who actually carries out that task.
2. **Authority:** This is the decision-making part of the job. If you have authority, you decide how the job is done. For example, if you are assigned to produce a report, you decide its content, structure, presentation and so on.
3. **Accountability:** This is the 'who carries the can' part of the job. If you are accountable, then, no matter who actually carries out the task, you retain full accountability for it if it goes wrong. So, if the report is inaccurate, you have to take the blame even if you didn't write it.

Effective delegation happens when someone is given a certain job to do (i.e. responsibility) and is allowed the freedom and authority to carry out the job in the way they think is best. That's not to say that there aren't limits to authority, of course, but individuals should be given as much authority as is reasonably possible.

One thing you cannot delegate is accountability – as the manager of the team, you are accountable for what your team members do and how well they do it. This is why many managers get very nervous about delegating – because they are the ones who 'carry the can'. Delegation does involve taking a bit of a calculated risk, but, if you get the process right, you minimise the possibility of things going horribly wrong!

To summarise, make sure that:

- you are aware of any training and development needs before delegating a task – don't set people up to fail because they don't have the right skills and you haven't taught them;
- the individual understands the broad parameters of the task, such as timescales, resources available to them and expected standard of performance;
- the person is enthusiastic about the delegated task, which they will be if you make it clear that you are not dumping an unwanted job on them but have instead chosen them because you think they'll do a great job and because you trust them and want to develop them.

Brief and communicate

The third key action is briefing and communication; however, as I cover these elements throughout the book (because they're so important!), I won't be discussing them again here. For example, see page 51 for things you need to consider to ensure you communicate with your team effectively; page 74 onwards on how consulting people and keeping them in the loop forms a crucial part of the planning process; page 113 on how you can improve the way you listen to other people; and page 52 for advice on how to both provide positive feedback and raise concerns about a team member's performance.

Monitor and support

A key part of getting the job done – and, therefore, of your role as a leader – is to make sure that tasks are finished, done to the right standard and completed within the timeframe allocated. To this end, one of the things you need to do is to monitor what is going on in the team and provide support, where necessary. I use the word 'monitor' advisedly. I think the word 'check' has connotations of a lack of trust, which I don't think is useful in developing people.

There's an old saying about how people prioritise work: first they do the things the manager monitors, then the things they like doing, then the things that absolutely have to be done! There's an element of truth in this old adage – no one wants their manager to think they're not doing what they're supposed to be doing. However, there are ways of monitoring and supporting people that avoid team members feeling like their manager is constantly looking over their shoulder. This gives team members the freedom to spread their time across the whole range of tasks they need to do, rather than putting all of their efforts into the tasks their manager is particularly focused on.

That being said, most people, especially if they are doing a job for the first time, are likely to make mistakes. Very few people manage to go from A to B without having a few mishaps. The following diagram illustrates what happens if you don't regularly monitor your team members. Things can go off track very quickly, but absolute catastrophe can be avoided if you're regularly keeping an eye on how things are going.

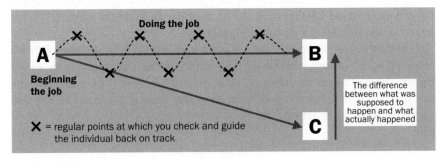

When you regularly catch up with your team members about how they're getting on, you can spot any massive deviations from the course early and help to correct them. It's much more effective to nudge people as they go along than to ignore them until the task is complete and then have to say it hasn't been done correctly or needs to be done again! Your job is to work alongside your team members so that they get to the end of the task successfully. This is much more motivating and, by the way, more effective!

Here are some tips for giving feedback as you go along:

1. Aim for a culture of 'appreciative enquiry'. This means that you look first for what is going well and then see what could be done differently.
2. Don't fix people's mistakes for them. Get them to identify the mistake themselves and then ask them what they could do differently in the future.
3. Make sure you find lots to praise – sincerely! Look for what is going well or is really good.
4. When the job gets done well – which it will if you've managed the process right – make sure you acknowledge that it has been done well, not just to the individual but to the rest of the team. There is nothing so motivating as success!

Evaluate

It makes me laugh that folk will forensically analyse in the minutest detail anything that went wrong but largely ignore why it is that some things went right. It is so important to evaluate your work and tasks – not just the big, clever projects but the day-to-day ones too. By taking time to think about what you did well and what you could have done differently, you not only anchor learning but also, more importantly, make sure you consciously replicate what works.

Evaluation doesn't have to be a lengthy, drawn-out process. At a weekly meeting, you can include an item on the agenda where for about ten minutes you simply share what went well in the previous week, or what went well in a particular task. Evaluation also gives you a great opportunity to praise folk!

How do you know if you're getting it right?

But how do you, as the leader, know that you are on the right track? What are the self-referencing mechanisms that can help you to know whether you're largely doing the right things at the right time?

I designed the following questionnaire as a handy aide-memoire for checking with yourself whether or not you are doing what's necessary to get the job done. The actual scores you give yourself are less important than the fact that they will guide you into what areas you may be doing less well at and therefore need to concentrate on.

Manager self-assessment: how well do the following statements describe you?

For each statement, give yourself a score from 1 (strongly disagree) to 10 (strongly agree).

1   I am clear what the purpose of my job as a manager is.

Low				Medium					High
1	2	3	4	5	6	7	8	9	10

2   I know what the organisation expects of me as a manager.

Low				Medium					High
1	2	3	4	5	6	7	8	9	10

3   I know how my job contributes to delivery of the organisation's objectives.

Low				Medium					High
1	2	3	4	5	6	7	8	9	10

4   I know when I'm doing a good job.

Low				Medium					High
1	2	3	4	5	6	7	8	9	10

5   When facing conflicting priorities, I always know what to do.

Low				Medium					High
1	2	3	4	5	6	7	8	9	10

6   My team members know what is expected of them.

Low				Medium					High
1	2	3	4	5	6	7	8	9	10

7   My team members know how their jobs contribute to the whole organisation.

Low				Medium					High
1	2	3	4	5	6	7	8	9	10

8   My team members always know what to prioritise.

Low				Medium					High
1	2	3	4	5	6	7	8	9	10

9   My team members are given direct feedback when they have done a good job.

Low				Medium					High
1	2	3	4	5	6	7	8	9	10

10   I regularly remind my team of the overall organisation's purpose.

Low				Medium					High
1	2	3	4	5	6	7	8	9	10

When it comes down to it, both you and your team will achieve some tasks brilliantly, some averagely well and some not well at all. And there will be things you fail at. The important thing is to recognise that not everything can, or will, go according to plan – that's a normal part of life. Keep a sense of perspective, a sense of humour and a sense of direction, and all will be well.

And keep the following diagram in mind!

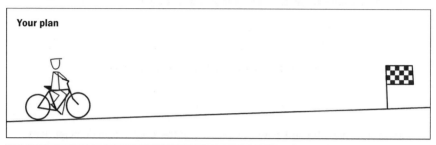

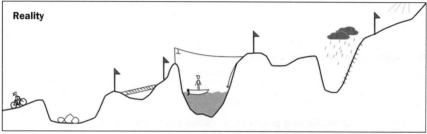

Remember

1. It's the process of planning that matters the most – not the piece of paper.
2. Involving people in developing the plan makes it much more likely you will achieve it.
3. Things *will* go wrong – it's how you respond to these instances that matters.

7 Time management

It is not that we have so little time but that we lose so much. ... The life we receive is not short but we make it so; we are not ill provided but use what we have wastefully.
Lucius Annaeus Seneca, *On the Shortness of Life*

If there is one thing that all people at work moan about, it's time. Never that there's too much of it, of course! Always that there is too little. The problem is that we rarely take responsibility for our own management of time. We tend to view our challenges with time management as the fault of something or someone else: we need better equipment, we should have less work to do, people shouldn't interrupt us and so on.

It's worse when you're the manager, because you are not only responsible for your own time management but also for how well your team members manage their time, their workloads and their stress.

In my experience, however, complaints about lack of time are rarely the result of there really being too much to do. I think such complaints are often used as a cover for inefficient working methods, lack of planning or forethought, or delays and failure to meet agreed deadlines. If you find your workload is overwhelming you, I promise you, the problem is much less likely to be with the volume of the work and much more likely to be about how you are managing it.

Time and workload management essentially comes down to two things: systems and processes that help, and the discipline to stick to them. There are no magic wands, I'm afraid.

When you look at time holistically, you may be quite surprised at how much or how little (depending on your perspective) you have available to you. I find it useful to look at time as if it were a budget, because that helps me to make better decisions about what to spend my time on. In the following table, I break down what is probably a fairly typical use of hours for someone in full-time work, who has about an hour's journey to work each day and who sleeps for around seven hours a night.

Time available

Amount of time (hours)	What does this number mean?	Notes
700,800	Total number of hours in your lifetime	Based on an average lifespan of 80 years
8,760	Total number of hours in a year	Based on 365 days a year (rather than 366 days in a leap year)
2,317.75	Hours spent asleep in a year	Based on the 6.35 hours a night that people in the UK sleep on average, according to the Sleep Council.
6,442.25	Hours spent awake in a year	Based on the total number of hours in a year minus the hours spent asleep
17.65	Hours spent awake each day	Based on the 6.35 hours a night.
1,768	Hours spent at work in a year	Based on a working year of 221 days (not including holidays, weekends or bank holidays) for 8 hours per day
1,835.6	Hours available at the weekend in a year	Based on 17.65 hours spent awake per day for 2 days per week, 52 weeks per year
2,132.65	Hours during the working week when not working and not asleep, in a year	Based on 9.65 hours spent awake and not working per day for 221 days per year

442	Hours spent travelling to work	Based on an average of 1 hour each way for 221 days per year
1,690.65	Hours available during the working week when not asleep, working or travelling, in a year	Based on 7.65 hours spent awake and not working or travelling per day for 221 days per year
38.25	Hours available during the working week when not asleep, working or travelling	Based on 7.65 hours per day for 5 days per week

When you consider that in any one week (not including weekends) you only have about 38 hours of spare time, which is 7.6 hours a day (of which at least a couple of hours are probably spent preparing or eating food, or doing basic chores – leaving approximately only 5.5 hours) what different choices might you make about how you spend your time?

Above all, what this table illustrates is that, given that it is physically impossible to actually make more time, we need to make the best of the time we have available to us.

The psychology of time

I came across a recent survey of office workers which looked at what gets in the way of people's productivity. The research looked at what people were wasting time on at work. The most common distractions, ranked in order, were:

1. cell phone/texting;
2. browsing the internet;
3. gossip;
4. social media;
5. colleagues dropping by;
6. smoke or snack breaks;
7. email;
8. meetings;
9. noisy co-workers;
10. sitting in a cubicle.

The survey was conducted in the US; however, I am sure that these findings are a pretty good reflection of any standard office environment. Bear in mind that some of these distractions might not be real problems, depending on the circumstances and your perceptions. For example, there are probably very good reasons why you and your colleagues have to attend meetings, even if it seems like a bit of a waste of time. Similarly, catching up with your colleagues is incredibly important to keep good relationships (see chapter 9 on page 107 for more on that) and, therefore, might not be a bad thing overall.

I find it interesting that, although we complain about time and how valuable it is, we don't generally behave as if it is a valuable commodity. Take, for example, how carefully we plan to spend our money; in contrast, we don't tend to do the same when deciding how we spend our time. If someone stole £50 off you in the street, you'd probably give chase, but if someone steals 50 minutes of your time, you probably tend to just let it go. This is mainly because we intuitively think of time as infinite, even though we know that it isn't. If you were told that you had won £1 million on the lottery (probably not quite enough to stop working altogether but a nice amount anyhow), it's likely that most of us would spend a fair bit of it on luxury items that we didn't really need. However, if we were given £1 million and told that it was all the money we would ever have for the rest of our lives, we would be much more likely to be more cautious about how we spent it.

Life's a bit like that. We have, on average, probably around 80 years to live. There is no more time (in this life, at least). Yet, we take the time we have for granted, spending it willy-nilly, without really thinking about how best to spend this precious gift.

Think again about how you budget your money. You know exactly how much money you are going to get at the end of the month in your salary; how much you must set aside for rent or your mortgage, bills and food (i.e. things you *have* to pay for); and, therefore, how much you can afford to spend on luxury items, such as a new frock or a holiday. If in any one month you get an unexpectedly large bill, you adjust your spending accordingly. (And, for the smart alecs among you: even if you use a credit card, you still have to pay it back at some point, plus there are no credit cards for extending life!)

Budgeting time is very similar to budgeting money. You will have things that you have to do – let's call them 'time mortgages' – and things that you'd like to do, which we can think of as 'time luxuries'. You can free up time by drawing a distinction between the two and making conscious decisions about them.

I suspect we are fairly good at budgeting time properly when it concerns our personal lives but forget all our good habits when we set foot in the office door! For example, if you are going on holiday and need to catch a plane, you will probably allow yourself extra time to get to the airport, in case there are delays en route. Similarly, if you are having friends around for dinner, you'll mentally plan what time you need to start cooking and when you plan to shower and change, and so on. What we are doing in such cases is thinking ahead. But how often do we turn up at work without a clear plan of what needs to be accomplished that day – just an expectation that 'we'll get on with stuff'?

One final point about the psychology of time management, before I go into specific tips and ideas to help manage your own and others' workloads: if you can eliminate bad habits around how you deal with time and create good ones instead, you will find time much easier to manage. For example, it's probably not the best habit to stop what you're doing as soon as an email arrives. A far better habit might be to deal with your emails first, and then switch off your email client so that you don't get distracted by pings and bleeps. Another daily habit could be to stop working to get yourself a coffee at, say, 11am and then 'walk the job' (see page 22) with your team until it's cool enough to drink. Alternatively, you could get into the habit of walking the job with your team to monitor progress and keep spirits up at 4pm – when motivation may be low but you can see all the results from the day (and get lots of opportunities to praise!). Create some good time habits that serve you.

Planning and prioritising for yourself and your team

You were employed to manage a team in order to deliver a set of objectives that support the ability of your organisation to deliver its vision. The job wasn't created for you out of charity! You are, therefore, being judged by the outcomes you and your team produce. There are always parts of any job that aren't directly linked to what you are measured on, but you may have to do them in order to get the job done. For example, you probably have to attend meetings, but attendance at meetings is not what you will be measured on at the end of the year. Your boss is probably not going to say, 'Well done, Sam. You didn't meet budget but you did attend 75 meetings this year!'

How do you decide what to prioritise? Well, this is where your time mortgages and time luxuries (see page 86) come in. There are a range of different things that you will be expected to do at work, but they don't all have the same value. With some things, if you don't do them, you might end up losing your job (for example, if you're responsible for running a telephone helpline and the phones don't get answered!). Others you need to do because they are part of some internal procedure which helps the whole organisation to run more smoothly (for example, producing a monthly report on call statistics or attending a monthly team meeting), but the world won't end if they don't get done. And then there are things that simply aren't important but that you end up doing because they somehow arrived on your desk (for example, responding to the round-robin email about the dirty cups left in the staff kitchen).

Learning to differentiate between the different types of task that you are expected to carry out at work is the first step towards planning and prioritising effectively. It's just like at home, where there are some jobs you have to do (such as washing up and cooking) and others that you don't have to do but feel you ought to (such as clearing out the attic).

You need to be absolutely clear about what parts of your job are 'must do', 'ought to do', 'could do' and 'don't have to do'. The same applies to your team members and their tasks – it's your role to make sure they are able to tell the difference and categorise their work. Don't accept the premise that 'everything's a priority' because, clearly, that's not true. Some things are simply more important than others. Plan those in and make time for the next priorities on the list.

Reactive and proactive tasks

I have a very simple approach to time management, with the acronym LITRW. That stands for 'live in the real world'! In the real world things go wrong: computers crash, photocopiers jam, people miss deadlines, trains run late, your inbox gets clogged up with junk email ... The world is messy and unpredictable – the best-laid plans and so on! However, if you remember this when you are organising your and your team's tasks, then you can often avoid rushing work or being stressed and anxious because a deadline is looming.

Most tasks can be broken down into those that are **proactive** and those that are **reactive**. **Proactive tasks** are those for which we can plan in advance. We know, for example, that the last day of every month is month end and that we need to notify the accounts team of any outstanding invoices or accruals (see page 97 for explanations of financial terms). Once we know, we can set aside time in our diary for that work. We also know that, inevitably, things will crop up unexpectedly during that day and that we need to make sure that we keep some time clear so that, if something does crop up, we don't miss our deadlines. I don't mean 'keep clear' in the sense that you just sit there twiddling your thumbs waiting for something to go wrong! There's always work to be done. What I mean is not scheduling long meetings or other deadlines for the same day.

Reactive tasks are those that you can't anticipate but you know will happen. The trick is, when you are planning your work, to leave time for things to go wrong. Don't leave it until the day of the deadline to write the report. Plan to do it a few days in advance so that if something unexpected crops up, you've still given yourself a reasonable chance of meeting the deadline.

You will have a sense of how much proactive and reactive time you have available. For example, you might find that on average about 60% of your week is spent dealing with reactive tasks and 40% with proactive ones. Plan your week accordingly, leaving plenty of time for things to go wrong. This method is not guaranteed to avoid crises, but it gives you a better chance of remaining in control.

Importantly, never leave things to the last minute! You're asking for trouble that way. You know that Sod's Law will break the photocopier just as you are frantically photocopying the minutes for the meeting you're due at in ten minutes. Live in the real world!

Making the best use of the resources available

In my experience, people are generally not that good at making the most of the basic resources they have available. You probably have Outlook or some other electronic diary system. There are so many features and functions in these electronic diaries that can help you to plan and manage your time, such as colour coding, task reminders and shared diary access among many, many others! Take some time to learn what they can do for you to make your life easier.

Most folk typically use their diary to remind them of appointments or meetings, or, occasionally, things that they don't want to forget, such as a birthday or an anniversary. This is, of course, immensely helpful to make sure we keep commitments we've made to see people but there is so much more you can do with a diary than just that.

One example is to use your diary to make commitments to yourself. You can make appointments with yourself to do certain pieces of work so you don't have to rely on your memory.

Below is a snippet of a typical week for me. I've obviously changed the names and organisations to protect individuals' privacy but the snippet is real. The key points to get out of these examples are:

- I have made appointments with myself to do tasks as well as left blank spaces for things that crop up – the reactive tasks. During the time allowed for reactive tasks, I get on with whatever is in my inbox or on my desk.
- My diary is open to all my staff members so they can see what I'm up to (although, if there are confidential things, I do mark them as private) – this is so that they don't waste time trying to find out where I am or what I am doing.
- Appointments are colour coded (although, obviously, here they are reproduced in black and white). I colour code separately for one-to-ones, management meetings, trustee meetings, speeches, external functions and so on. This makes it easy for me to see, at a glance, how much time I'm spending externally with DSC's beneficiaries and how much time I'm spending on internal meetings, so that I have a good sense of whether I'm spending time on my priorities. Too much of certain colours means too much internal focus; plenty of other colours means I'm out and about serving our charities.

	MONDAY	TUESDAY	WEDNESDAY	THURSDAY	FRIDAY
	18	19	20	21	22
			Auditors at DSC		
	Reminder: NCVO Conference (Neil and Ruth attending)	**Reminder:** PA (Simon) working from home all day if I need him. **Reminder:** get in touch with R.B. to arrange a meeting	**Reminder:** IT engineers' check-ups today (make sure all departments are aware)	**Reminder:** bring suitcase with papers for the NEETs conference	**Private:** take Mabel to the vet
09	**Self appointment:** working from home. Preparation time for speeches ('Effective Training for NEETs' conference speech and 'Soldiering On Awards' speech) + Q1 from Trustees' Report (Debra Allcock Tyler)		**External meeting:** Strategic Network Development Committee Meeting @ Mary-at-Hill, City, London	**Speech:** 'Effective Training for NEETs' conference @ TeachSport office, Catford, London	**Self appointment:** work on Mark's appraisal (Debra Allcock Tyler)
10		**Self appointment:** prepare team briefing (Debra Allcock Tyler)			**Private:** meet Charlie
11		**Internal meeting:** 1-1 with Amanda (Amanda)			
12		**Travel reminder:** 12.10pm travel to lunch, Euston Road	**Self appointment:** revisit 'Effective Training for NEETs' conference speech (Debra Allcock Tyler)		**Self appointment:** keep free prep time for meeting with Omar (Debra Allcock Tyler)
13		**External meeting:** lunch with CEO of JDRF @ Prezzo restaurant, Euston Road	**Internal meeting:** 1-1 lunch with Fred (Fred)		**Management meeting:** meet with Omar to finalise strategy stuff (Omar)
14		**Travel reminder:** 14.15pm travel back from Euston Road			
15	**Private:** dentist	**Internal meeting:** 1-1 with Dan (Financial Papers) (Dan)		**Travel reminder:** travel to the office	
16				**Management meeting:** Leadership Team meeting	
17		**Trusteeship commitment:** Community Foundation strategy presentation			**Trusteeship commitment:** Whiteknights School opening of new playground – me to cut the ribbon
18					

Making appointments with yourself to do specific work has plenty of advantages:

- You don't have to remember what needs to be done – it's in the diary!
- If things change, you can easily move the task to a day or time when you can do it.
- Other people looking in your diary can see when you are busy and can make an informed decision about when it's best to contact you.
- It encourages you to look ahead and think realistically about deadlines – you have to plan the work in advance and will notice if you are overcommitting on certain days.
- It helps you to prioritise tasks that matter over those that aren't so important.

I would encourage you to advise your team members to operate the same system – not least because it's also a way in which you can monitor their workload and offer support or guidance, if necessary. Open diaries are particularly effective: just as people can look at your diary to find out whether you're available and what you're doing, you and your team members can look at another team member's diary to see where they are. Instead of having to ask everybody who is around where someone is, you can look in that person's diary and see that they are at a meeting, for example. This saves loads of time when you are answering the phone on behalf of somebody else, too – you don't waste time hunting the person down and you can be more helpful to the caller by being able to tell them when the individual is going to be back at their desk to return their call. This is so much more professional – rather than simply saying 'I'm sorry, Freddie is not available', you can say 'I'm sorry, Freddie is in a staff briefing at the moment but should be back at his desk by 11.30. I'll ask him to call you then.'

The other trick with diary management is to estimate how long you think a task will take and then allow extra time. For instance, if you think a task should take an hour, put it in at 2pm but schedule the next thing for 3.30pm, instead of 3pm. That way, if the task takes longer than an hour, it doesn't matter because you've planned for it. And, if it does take the full hour, well, then you've gained half an hour that you didn't have and can do something else with it!

Using a diary this way will help you to draw your team members' attention to how they are using their time and help them to make intelligent decisions about the deadlines they agree to, so that they can realistically meet those deadlines without affecting the rest of their work.

Rolling to-do list

Extending the notion of making appointments with yourself to do tasks, I would suggest you get into the habit of using a to-do list. Most electronic diary systems allow this in the form of a task list, although not everyone finds that this particular method suits them. For your to-do list you can equally use a dated notebook, your electronic diary or a reminder list. The main thing is that, instead of writing down a daily or weekly list of things to do and then moving things from one list to another, you write down what you have to do on the day *on which you intend to do it*! This is similar to making appointments with yourself in your diary to do tasks, except that in the diary you would generally make appointments to do 'big' tasks, whereas the rolling to-do list would generally contain fairly small, quick jobs, such as telephone a colleague, check an invoice, chase someone up for something they've promised you and so on.

For example, let's say today is Monday and you get an email from a colleague asking you to phone them about a service user, when you have time. It's not urgent. You haven't got time to do it right away, but you know you've got time on Wednesday so you make a note in your diary or dated notebook on the day on which you intend to make the call.

You can then completely forget about the request, because, when you get to Wednesday and open your diary or rolling to-do book, you will be automatically reminded. If you find you can't complete the task on the day you have it written, you can simply move it to a day when you can.

It's also a good idea to have a rolling to-do list for team tasks. If you've got the space, a whiteboard on the wall, marked into days of the week, is a great place for leaving messages about things that need to be done on certain days.

Managing deadlines

Every day at work, especially as a manager, you are either setting or agreeing to deadlines. Everybody has them and they do matter! Some deadlines are obvious: they occur because a job needs to happen, by a certain date, in order for something else to happen. For example, it might be that all invoices need to be submitted to the accounts team by the end of the month so that they can be processed. Other deadlines are arbitrary or self-imposed. For example, you might set a deadline for everyone to tidy up their bit of the server. Sometimes, these self-imposed ones are particularly important, such as when the server must be cleaned up because you're transferring to a new system. Otherwise, there may be no particular urgency but the job needs to get done at some point so you set a deadline to keep yourself and your team on track.

The main problem with deadlines is that either we are unrealistic in our belief about whether we can meet them or we agree to them without really thinking through the implications. So often we agree to deadlines because we want to be seen to be co-operative, even if we don't think we can meet them. We say things like 'I'll try'. The problem is that people don't remember you said you'd try – they remember that you didn't meet the deadline.

To make managing deadlines easier, remember some simple rules:

- Do not agree to deadlines you know you can't meet.
- Explain why you can't meet the deadline. Don't just say you're too busy – explain what it is that you're doing and why that is more important than the job you're being asked to do.
- Offer an alternative deadline – one that you can meet.
- If negotiating the deadline is not acceptable, negotiate the resources you need to get the job done.

For example:

> **Debra:** Ben, can you get the risk assessment done by Friday 5pm?
>
> **Ben:** No, sorry Debra. I've got to get the funding application in by Friday morning, otherwise we'll miss the deadline. I could get it done by 5pm next Tuesday.
>
> **Debra:** That's too late, it needs to be sent to the trustees by Monday morning at the latest.
>
> **Ben:** OK, well, if you could ask Jay if he can spare time to help with the funding application, I might be able to do it. Or I could email the trustees for you and explain that it will be coming late because I'm working on funding.
>
> **Debra:** I'll talk to Jay first. If he can't help, then, yes, good idea, we'll email the trustees about the delay.

Of course, these rules are not guaranteed to work every time, but they give you a better chance of both meeting the deadline and conveying to your manager or colleagues that you're co-operative and that you meet deadlines that you've agreed to.

Ten tips for deadline management

1. Whenever you're asked to agree to a deadline, first check in your diary and/or rolling to-do list to decide whether you can realistically set aside enough time to achieve it.

2. When setting (or agreeing to) a deadline, *never* use the words 'as soon as possible'. They are meaningless, really, because they indicate that you have absolutely no idea how important the task is in relation to other tasks. As a result, the person to whom you are giving the deadline is less likely to prioritise it effectively. Offer a *specific* date and time with a *reason* for the deadline so that your colleagues and team members understand the consequences of missing the deadline. For example, 'I need this by Tuesday 12.30pm because I have to get it to the treasurer by 5pm before she leaves for a two-week holiday.'

3. When you receive something marked 'ASAP', pick up the phone and ask the sender when they *actually* need the job done by and what the consequences of missing the deadline are.

4. Similar rules apply to the word 'urgent'. How urgent is 'urgent'? Immediately? Today? By the end of the week? Be specific.

5. When sending out something that you need a response to, always give a deadline for the response and, again, a reason for the deadline.

6. When leaving phone messages, give a deadline for the action you need and explain why the deadline exists. This makes it more likely that the deadline will be met and will avoid the person calling you back to clarify when you need the action done by.

7. Never leave it to the last minute to chase someone about a deadline. You know that you haven't received whatever it is you requested, so it's highly likely it hasn't been done! By chasing at the point of the deadline, it is likely that you will end up cross and the other person defensive. Make a note in your rolling to-do list to chase in advance. However, ...

8. ... let people know that you will be chasing them in advance. You can do this politely, by saying something like 'I'll give you a quick call on Monday afternoon to see how you're getting on and if there are any problems.'

9. Never leave it to the last minute to deliver on a deadline that you've agreed to. Get the job done ahead of time, if at all possible.

10. If you are likely to miss a deadline, don't wait until you've actually missed it before telling the person who requested your help. The moment you know you can't meet the deadline, ring the person who's waiting to receive the job, explain why you can't complete it on time and offer a new deadline.

Ruthless with time, kind to people

Most of the jobs you'll do at work involve getting results through other people, especially when you are the manager. You have to deal with all sorts of folk: colleagues, team members, service users, funders, other staff, volunteers, directors, trustees and so on. Every interaction you have with them will influence how well you can do your job and how well they can do theirs.

Effective time management is heavily reliant on relationships. If people trust you to do what you said you would, they are much less likely to keep chasing you for things. If you trust them to do what they said they would, you are less likely to need to use precious time chasing them.

It's important to recognise that something you might not see as particularly productive – the time that you spend chatting with colleagues about non-work stuff – is, in fact, very valuable, because taking the time to chat helps to build positive relationships. Once you have a positive relationship, you are more likely to work effectively with that individual, so take time out to learn about your colleagues and what matters to them, both personally and professionally. In addition, it makes for a much nicer working environment if you know and care about your colleagues.

Here are some tips on how to build good working relationships:

- Get to know people face to face – visit them in their own department.
- Instead of emailing or phoning, pop in to see your team as often as is sensible.
- Whenever you visit another department, don't just head straight for the person you want to talk to – take time to say a general hello to others as you pass.
- Smile and thank people if they do something for you – even if it's expected of them as part of their job. People will want to work with or for someone who they believe appreciates their effort.
- If you see someone from another department visiting your own, make an effort to greet them with a warm smile and a hello.
- All departments in an organisation are there for a reason. It's rare that one department is more important than another. Make sure others know that you understand the importance of their work.
- Find out what other departments' or managers' problems are and see whether there is anything you can do in your own work or with your own team to make the other folks' lives easier. For example, make sure you meet any deadlines that they set for you.
- Be honest without being unhelpful or impolite. If you can't help, say so – but give good reasons and offer alternatives that might help. By all means, say no. But don't leave it at that – see if there are other ways you could help.

Good relationships at work take time and energy to achieve. And they can be ruined with a hastily or badly worded email, a flippant remark, or a missed deadline. Taking the time to make sure you are communicating what you need effectively is worth doing. Below are some simple things to remember when dealing with other folk.

Action	Remember
Making a request	■ Be pleasant but direct and to the point ■ Explain why you are making the request ■ Explain the importance of the request and the consequences of it not being met ■ Keep it short ■ Don't manipulate ■ Don't personalise the request (for example, don't use phrases such as 'you owe me') ■ Be prepared for the person to say no, and have a plan B ■ Smile!
Refusing a request	■ Show empathy and understanding of the request ■ Be clear that you can't comply – use the word 'no' ■ Explain why you can't comply ■ If you can, offer alternative suggestions ■ Don't personalise the refusal (for example, don't use phrases such as 'no, because you didn't help me')
Gathering information	■ Explain why you need the information ■ Give a deadline, if necessary ■ Ask open questions ■ Listen ■ Don't interrupt ■ Don't feel the need to respond verbally to every statement the other person makes

Giving information	<ul><li>Don't just begin giving details without asking the other person whether now is convenient</li><li>Be clear about why you are giving the information – what is the purpose?</li><li>Be direct and to the point</li><li>Summarise</li><li>If you need the information to be acted upon, be clear about what outcome you want and what the deadline is</li><li>Listen</li></ul>
If you disagree with someone	<ul><li>Look for areas of agreement first</li><li>Objectively state the area of disagreement</li><li>Don't personalise (for example, don't use phrases such as 'you would think that, wouldn't you?')</li><li>Listen</li><li>Show that you understand the other person's viewpoint, even though you don't agree with it</li><li>Disagree with what is being said – not the person saying it</li><li>Be prepared to change your opinion</li><li>Say you're wrong, if you are</li><li>Negotiate a positive solution for both people</li></ul>

Much of time management is really basic common sense. There aren't any magic wands – it's all about good habits.

Remember

1. Live in the real world and plan for things to go wrong.
2. Communicate the reasons for and the consequences of deadlines.
3. Build up strong relationships with your colleagues.

8 Understanding the money

Finance is the heart in a charity body – it's incredibly difficult for the body to function without it.
Caron Bradshaw, CEO, Charity Finance Group and Chair, DSC

Once you've become a manager, you will, possibly for the first time, have to demonstrate a decent understanding of how the organisation's finances function and how the work of you and your team contributes to the financial picture of your organisation. You may also be responsible for managing a budget – income or expenditure, or possibly both. If you are not used to working with charity accounts, it is easy to feel intimidated.

Charity finance, however, is fairly straightforward on a day-to-day basis. If it ever gets complex, it's usually at year end, when the accounts are being done and the auditors and your accounts team or treasurer get into arguments about whether something is a fixed or tangible asset, an administration cost or fundraising cost, or restricted or unrestricted funds. You probably won't get involved in those sorts of debates (although they are good fun!).

Trust your finance team

I strongly recommend you build up a good relationship with your finance team – it will pay off. I remember, many years ago, I had to report on the financial performance of a team that I was accountable for to the organisation's senior management. My team managed the major accounts, so we had to track all the income from every source, even if that income had been generated by another team. Because we were measured on the *total* income from all of the companies to which we sold, regardless of who in our organisation had brought in the money, that's what we reported. However, some of the members of the senior management team thought that my team and I were trying to take credit for others' sales, and every meeting one particular manager challenged our results, saying we were misreporting. Apparently, she'd never been that happy about our team being set up in the first place. I was starting to get really pissed off about it, to be honest.

Then, my very clever boss suggested that I pre-empt the inevitable next month's challenge. I followed her advice and the week before our meeting I made an appointment with our director of finance and asked him to check that my figures were right, that I was not misreporting and that the figures could legitimately be presented in the way that they were. He looked them over and said that yes, everything was as it should be. At the next meeting, when my fellow manager yet again challenged my report, I simply referred her questions to the director of finance, who said our figures were absolutely right. She had nowhere to go after that! And she never raised the issue again. I suspect that this was not because she agreed we were right but because she couldn't disagree with our finance director. Ha!

Managing your budget

Budgets are fairly straightforward as long as you establish the key elements. First, you need to understand whether yours is just an expenditure budget or if you have income targets too. Then, importantly, you need to identify how much authority you have over your budget. If you don't have sufficient authority to make decisions about what you spend and don't spend, then you can quite legitimately argue that you can't be held accountable for the budget.

In a charity, you also need to know whether any parts of your budget consist of restricted funds, which means you are limited in what you can spend that money on. In fact, you can only spend it on those activities for which it was given by the donor. All of this can be clarified with your finance team or your own line manager.

It's not likely you will have substantial sums at your disposal, but you may well have access to petty cash. Petty cash is just actual money, usually kept in a locked tin, that you can use for small or urgent purchases. However, you still have to account for it by keeping receipts and reconciling how much you've spent on what with what's left in the tin.

Petty cash is notoriously hard to keep a track of because it is dipped into for all kinds of expenses from bottles of milk to Blu-Tack to hold your computer together, so it's important you keep an eye on it.

Terminology

Many folk say that as soon as financial terms start getting mentioned, their brains freeze over. My advice is not to let the jargon intimidate you. It's just language, after all. You probably know that the French word for 'hello' is 'bonjour'. Well, the 'accountance' term for the 'profit and loss sheet' in the charity sector is 'SoFA', which stands for 'statement of financial activities'. 'Accountance' for 'profit' is 'surplus'. And so on. 'Accountance', of course, isn't a word – but I'm going to use it anyway!

The main focus of this chapter is to give you some basic explanation of terms you are likely to come across in your day-to-day work. I'm going to keep the explanations as simple as is reasonable – sufficient for you to have a good enough understanding of the terms to be competent in your new role. There will be terms which I have not included in this chapter (mainly because if you need to know them, then you probably need more formal training than reading a chapter in a book!).

If you are ever in doubt, *do not be afraid to ask*! I promise you that your finance team (or your finance person, if your organisation is not big enough to have a whole team) will be absolutely delighted to explain how finance works.

Definitions of terms

The following are the most common terms you will find in a standard set of charity accounts or hear being used by your finance team. Being familiar with these will help you feel more confident in your job and make dealing with financial matters easier.

Accrual

Accrual is the term used to describe an expenditure which you have incurred but for which you have not yet received the invoice, so it hasn't been paid but you know that it is coming. When you are asked to 'do your accruals', you are being asked to let your finance team or treasurer know about anything that you have spent money on in the month but that you have yet to receive the invoice for. This is so that the organisation knows how much it owes in any one month and can make sure it has enough cash to pay for it and run its finances effectively. Once you get the invoice, the finance team will adjust the accounts to reflect the real invoice value and take out the accrued amount.

Amortisation and depreciation

These terms refer to the fact that most assets lose value over time. Amortisation and depreciation mean essentially the same thing. However, while **amortisation** refers to intangible assets (see 'Asset' on page 100),

depreciation refers to tangible assets. For example, you generally sell your car for a lot less than you bought it for, because it is older and used. So over the years it loses value. This is also the case in organisations. To amortise or depreciate something simply means to spread the cost of the asset over the period of its usable life. This means that you don't show the full cost in the year the asset was acquired – you spread it over the number of years you feel the asset will be used and have value. Even though you may have used cash to pay for the asset in full, from an accounting point of view you spread the cost over more than one year and the amount left at the end of any year reflects what price you might be able to sell the asset for at that point in time.

Asset

An asset is a 'thing' an organisation owns that it could potentially sell, or anything that is owed to the organisation. Assets can be categorised into **tangible assets** and **intangible assets**.

Tangible assets include fixed assets (usually physical things such as a computer, photocopier, kettle, car or building) and current (or liquid) assets, such as actual cash in the bank, debts for which you can collect cash, and other things that you could potentially sell quickly for cash, for example short-term investments in bonds. They are called tangible assets because you can physically touch them.

Intangible assets include things like intellectual property, licences to provide services, and websites. They are called intangible assets because you can't physically touch them (see – quite logical, really!).

Balance sheet

A balance sheet is a statement of what the organisation owns, what it earns, what it owes and what is left over. The term 'balancing the books' comes from the balance sheet. This term means that all that you owe and all that you are owed have been matched up and make sense. It's a snapshot of the organisation at a given point in time – the same time each year – so that anyone reading it can compare it to previous years to see how the organisation is doing. Its purpose is primarily to show investors, funders and suppliers the financial state of the organisation so they can decide how financially viable it is and whether it is worth the risk of funding or giving supplies to.

Budget

It's probably safe to assume that you will have come across some sort of a budget and know that it is, essentially, an attempt to work out how much money the organisation is going to collect in the year and how much it is likely to spend, and, therefore, how much is going to be left over. By doing a budget, you are effectively making decisions about how you will deliver your charitable objects and what you can and cannot buy or spend in a year. So, if you think that you're going to bring in less money than you are planning to spend, you will either budget to bring in more or, more likely, decide what you are not going to buy or spend money on unless you happen to get more money in.

Budgets are often treated as if they are real things and people can get quite obsessed with them, but, really, they are always simply an educated guess. The reason they matter is because they effectively represent your planned expenditure for the coming year and how much money you need in order to fund that plan. You need to know how well you are doing against your budget so that, where you are not performing as expected, you can make good decisions about what to spend and what to cut during the year to make sure that the organisation stays viable. A budget is a bit like a map: it gives you a sense of where you are in relation to what you planned to do, and knowing that gives you options about what to do next.

Capital expenditure

The term 'capital expenditure' comes from 'capitalisation' (see next section) and relates to money that has been spent on equipment, property and other fixed assets which will have value over more than one financial year or accounting period.

Capitalisation

Capitalisation is the process of turning an expense (or series of expenses) into an asset or assets (see 'Asset' on page 100). You would tend to capitalise things like big, expensive bits of equipment, such as computers or photocopiers. To capitalise something means to spread the cost over the value of the thing. You might capitalise, say, something that costs È1,000 over four years and it would show as a depreciating asset on the balance sheet. So, for instance, in year one it would show as worth È1,000, in year two as È750, in year three as È500 and in year four as È250. In year five it would be worthless (i.e. in theory, you could no longer sell it, as no one would buy it because it's too old) and you would no longer show it as an asset on your balance sheet.

It is fairly easy to identify individual purchases (such as those described above) as assets, but what happens if creating the assets involves many small transactions? This is often the case with intangible assets, such as websites. Website creation involves web design, developer fees, staff time costs, graphic design costs, programming costs and so on; therefore, the finished website's asset cost will be built up of various individual expenses incurred over a period of time. Only when the website is finished and ready to go live does it become an asset, which has to be amortised over a number of years. So, to charge individual transactions as expenses in the SoFA (see page 105) at cost would be misleading the reader because then the asset's value would be accounted for in one year and in subsequent years you would not have any cost to charge. The honest thing to do in these situations is to remove the cost from the SoFA and accumulate it as an asset on your balance sheet.

Cash flow

Cash flow is the term used to describe the pattern and analysis of how cash is received and how it is spent over a particular period of time. The difference between cash received and cash spent is what you have in your bank account. In any organisation, cash flow is hugely important because you need money in the bank to pay bills.

Cash flow is *not* the same as reserves (see 'Free reserves (or general funds)' on page 103). At times you might have lots of cash and no reserves or lots of reserves and no cash. You may have money in your bank account simply because there are some bills you haven't paid yet, or because someone has paid you in advance (which often happens with funders).

Core costs

Core costs (sometimes referred to as administration costs) are an organisation's central administration and management costs, which are not necessarily directly linked to a particular project. For example, if you have an accountant, they will probably be described as a core cost. Other things classified as core costs could be the cost of renting your building, paying your energy bill or paying for the photocopier. Because these costs are often not directly attributable to a specific project, it can be difficult to get funding for them. However, they are a critical part of a charity's expenditure. All money spent in servicing the charity is delivering against the charity's objects. Don't fall into the trap of thinking that, just because something falls under administrative or core costs, it isn't money properly and appropriately spent in service of the organisation's beneficiaries. I personally hate the term core costs as I think it is misleading to donors. I prefer wording which allows fundraisers and other staff to explain the charity's needs (see 'Full cost recovery' on page 104, for example).

Cost centre

Accountants will often call a department a 'cost centre'. This is a discrete unit within the charity where money is generated and/or spent (so it will have some sort of budget allocated to it). For example, the volunteer team, the fundraising team, the outreach team and the finance team might each be a cost centre. Accountants analyse teams and departments in this way so that the organisation can see how effectively (or not, as the case may be) the finances associated with that particular department or team are being used. This allows the organisation to make decisions as to how the unit can manage its money more effectively, if necessary.

Creditor

Creditors are those people or organisations to whom *your organisation owes* money. Essentially, you have received a product or service from them which you haven't yet paid for, so they have technically extended you 'credit' (hence the term creditor). Alternatively, you may have borrowed actual money from a bank or individual.

The term creditor can also be used to refer to restricted funds, where someone or some organisation has given you money to spend on a particular thing (for example, a grant to develop a specific project) but you haven't done the work yet. Until the work is done, the donor or grant giver is effectively a creditor, because if you don't complete the work, you will have to give the money back. Until the work is done, you owe them the money.

The simplest way to remember that this term is about people to whom *you owe* money is to remember that if you have a credit card, you owe the credit card company money. Ergo 'creditors'.

Debtor

Debtors are those people or organisations who *owe you* money. They are in debt to you because you have given them a service or product and they are yet to pay for it.

Designated funds

A designated fund is one where your trustees have earmarked some money, usually from unrestricted funds (see 'Unrestricted fund' on page 106), to pay for a particular project or special purpose, but where they can change their minds about what to use it for. For example, you might designate funds to pay for a website upgrade later in the year. Then, if you find you can't afford it, you might un-designate the funds and use them for something else. Unlike restricted funds (see 'Restricted fund' on page 105), designated funds are entirely within the remit of the trustees to choose what to do with them.

Direct cost

A direct cost is one that is directly attributable to a cost centre (see 'Cost centre' on page 102) or other revenue line – i.e. there is a clear link between the nature of the cost and the team or department where it is incurred. For example, the direct cost of sending out funding applications might be the cost of postage, envelopes, the paper used and so on. (Compare with 'Indirect cost' on page 104.)

Free reserves (or general funds)

Free reserves are essentially the 'profit' or surplus that a charity has retained from its income-generating activities that is not earmarked for a particular project and that the charity can choose to do whatever it likes with. Free reserves can accumulate over time and the trustees can use them to invest in development within the charity or other activities that support the delivery of its charitable objects.

(In charities, we generally call an excess of income over expenditure a surplus to distinguish it from the term 'profit'. This is to emphasise and reinforce to funders and donors that charities do not have shareholders or owners to whom profits can be distributed and that surpluses can only be reinvested in the charity so as to help deliver its charitable objects.)

Free reserves are unrestricted and made up of cash as well as assets which could be turned into cash quickly (i.e. free reserves do not include fixed assets). To illustrate this, consider a new charity that starts life with a È1 million cash donation to use as it likes. This unrestricted donation means that the charity has an unrestricted reserve of È1 million cash, which is available to use immediately; hence it has a È1 million free reserve. If the charity then spends È600,000 to acquire a building, it still has reserves of È1 million, but the free reserves have been reduced to È400,000 (the value of the cash left). The È600,000 building cannot be made available to spend quickly, as it will take months (if not years) to sell the building and make the cash available to use, so the building cannot be included in the free reserves.

Some charities sit on a minimum amount of reserves in order to have rainy-day money in case a grant falls through or takes too long to be paid. However, charities are not encouraged to build up reserves without a good reason as money is given by donors and funders to charities to spend on their activities to serve beneficiaries.

Full cost recovery

Full cost recovery is a term that was adopted in the early part of the new millennium to help funders to understand that there are parts of charities which need to be funded but which do not necessarily form a direct part of the funded project. This could include overheads, such as rent and rates; salaries, such as those of the CEO or finance director; core costs (see 'Core costs' on page 102), such as rent of the premises; or equipment which is shared. It is not a technical accounting term but it is used to help explain the funding needs of a charity when it applies for a grant or a loan.

Indirect cost

An indirect cost is one that is indirectly attributable to a cost centre (see 'Cost centre' on page 102). For example, the finance team in the organisation costs money but doesn't generate revenue; therefore, the cost of running that team needs to be allocated across the organisation. So, a portion of that cost will be attributed to, say, the fundraising team and to the operations team, or the volunteer team. There isn't such a clear connection between the cost and the unit paying it as is the case with direct costs (see 'Direct cost' on page 103).

Liabilities (or current liabilities)

Liability is the term used to describe what you owe to other people or organisations for items that you have bought and not yet paid for, or money you have borrowed and not yet repaid. Grants received in advance of the expenditure for which they are destined also count as liabilities. This is because if, for some reason, you don't deliver the project or work that the grant was given for, then you have to pay the money back. The grant is no longer a liability as soon as you have spent it.

Management accounts

Management accounts are one of the most useful internal documents within any charity. They are usually produced monthly and show financial information which indicates actual progress against the budget. They often include forecasts and are the basis on which management makes decisions about future expenditure and revenue generation. They are used to set budgets, plan ahead and monitor the financial performance of the charity throughout the year.

Net current assets (or working capital)

Net current assets is the term used to describe the money that is available after current liabilities (what the organisation owes) have been deducted from current assets (what the organisation owns and has in the bank). What's left over is the money available for conducting the day-to-day operations of the organisation.

Prepayment

A prepayment is where you have paid for something, or someone has paid you for something, that has not yet been used. For example, a deposit on a venue or rent paid in advance. It can also refer to a payment for a service which has not been completely used up at a particular point in time (an example is a payment for one year of insurance when you pay for the whole year in advance).

Restricted fund

A restricted fund is formed when you are given a grant, loan or donation where the giver has specified that you may only use it for a certain purpose. Such money usually comes with conditions attached to it. Restricted funds are a major source of funding for many charities.

SoFA

SoFA is an acronym for 'statement of financial activities'. All organisations have to describe what they are doing with the money they receive and the money they spend. In the private sector this would be called a 'profit and loss account'. A SoFA is slightly different to company accounts in what it has to contain: unlike company accounts, charity accounts have to show where the various funds have come from and which of them are restricted (i.e. can only be spent on certain things). Essentially, a SoFA is a summary of what the charity generated in income, what it spent that money on and what is left over, if anything.

Stock

Stock is the term used to describe physical assets that can be sold, such as books, white goods and so on.

Unrestricted fund

The nirvana of all fundraisers, unrestricted funds are precious and increasingly rare! They are funds that have been given to the charity without any caveats, or that the charity has earned or accumulated itself from its own activities. The charity is free to spend them on whatever it wants, provided the activity is within the charitable objects.

Variance

Variance is the term used to describe the difference between what is planned and what actually happened. For example, if you planned to raise È5,000 and only raised È4,500, the variance would be a negative one of È500. Or, if you planned to spend È3,000 and only spent È1,000, the variance would be a positive one of È2,000.

Summary

Having a good understanding of the financial terms I have listed above should be sufficient to make sure you are financially literate enough to have a decent understanding of charity finance and to ask the right sorts of questions.

However, all organisations have their own ways of presenting and discussing financial information internally. Make sure you understand not just your own team's financial area – and most importantly what is expected of you – but also those of others. This will help you to make good decisions about what you do and don't do within your own team and ensure that you share the right sort of information at the right time with the finance team and the senior managers in your organisation, so that they can make new plans and adjust existing plans appropriately.

Remember

1. Financial information is just information that is there to help the organisation to do its work and serve its beneficiaries.
2. As a manager, you are now expected to understand basic finances – make sure you are familiar with how financial matters work in your organisation.
3. Never be afraid to ask if there is something you don't understand.

9 Creating good relationships

The most important single ingredient in the formula of success is knowing how to get along with people.
Attributed to Theodore Roosevelt, US president

The higher up the management ladder you climb, the more you will realise that a great deal of your ability to deliver your objectives and get the job done relies on how well you build and maintain good relationships – not just with your own team but also, critically, with your line manager and other managers in the organisation. There may be a time when you will also have to develop relationships with trustees in order to carry out your role effectively.

Realising that a large amount of your work as a manager consists of simply being nice and helpful to other people and spending time talking and listening to them may come as a bit of a surprise. When I was very junior in an organisation, some of the managers appeared to be spending more time chatting to each other or in (what seemed to me then) very unnecessary meetings than sat at their desks, or they just disappeared off for lunch together. I was suspicious and a bit cynical, if I'm honest. I, as most of my colleagues probably also did, assumed that they were having an easy ride and leaving us to do all the work. One of my managers in particular used to spend a lot of time hanging out with the marketing manager – I always thought it was because he quite fancied him. It was only years later I realised that, actually, that relationship was incredibly important in terms of my department getting its services higher up the marketing schedule; without that relationship, we wouldn't have achieved the results we needed. So my boss was doing his job, even though I didn't realise it at the time, and it was because we had such a good relationship with the marketing team that the team frequently did a bit more for us than it technically had to.

It's true that human beings like to do things for people they get on well with. Technically, we should deliver our work in the same way to everyone, simply because it's the professional thing to do and part of our job. However, we're still human and, even if we don't mean to, we're bound to prioritise our mates or those people whom we just get on better with.

Almost no one operates in isolation in an organisation. All of us, in one way or another, rely on others to help us to do our work. Spending time building relationships with others is a really important part of your job as a manager. There are three levels of relationship that you will spend most of your time thinking about: with your team members, with your colleagues and with your own boss.

What's different about your relationships with your team members when you're their manager?

This is how it goes. No matter how lovely a human being you are, you will not be able to have the same kind of relationship with the team that you manage that you had with your colleagues when you were part of a team, because you now have a different level of responsibility. No matter how well you get on with your team members, ultimately, it is hard for them to forget that you have the power to make their lives miserable. You are the one who carries out their appraisals, monitors their performance and allocates their tasks. And you are NOT PART OF THE TEAM – YOU ARE ITS LEADER! Yes, I've deliberately used capital letters to appear as if I'm shouting at you, because I am. It drives me loopy to hear apparent leadership gurus implicitly or explicitly suggest that you can have the same kind of relationship with your direct reports as you do with your management colleagues. On almost every occasion when I've seen managers attempting to remain part of the team, in the end, it caused issues: accusations of favouritism and disgruntled members of the team who felt that others were getting favourable treatment, or angry, upset employees who thought their manager was their friend and felt betrayed when they didn't get what they wanted or were asked to do something they didn't like.

Don't get me wrong – it is absolutely possible to have strong, warm and friendly relationships with folk who work for you, but you must remember that you need to 'share the love' with *all* members of the team. If people feel that they are being excluded or that other folk are in the know, it can create real resentment. Having said that, one of my very best friends is a former line manager of mine and, in fact, ended up working for me for a while. We got on brilliantly when I worked for her and when she worked for me, but I wouldn't have described us as best mates at the time. We created that real in-depth relationship once we stopped working together.

If you are managing your relationships with your direct reports well, you should find that every once in a while they moan about you. Don't be fooled, people do moan about their boss – it's normal. Your job is to make sure that their moans are trivial ones and not about serious problems that you haven't dealt with.

What makes a good relationship?

Good relationships have many features in common, whether they are professional relationships at work or personal ones with family, friends or neighbours. Much of what makes relationships good applies regardless of the relative statuses of the people involved. Some common characteristics of good relationships are that both people:

- trust each other;
- tell each other the truth – tactfully and constructively – where necessary;
- like each other and enjoy each other's company;
- have a good appreciation of each other's motivations;
- respect each other's values;
- don't hold grudges against each other;
- are willing to say sorry;
- are willing to accept an apology;
- accept that the other will make mistakes;
- don't blame one another;
- help each other out of tight spots;
- make an effort to talk to each other;
- keep each other informed;
- admit when they have made a mistake;
- ask for and offer help;
- joke with each other.

There are probably more.

You may well be looking at that list and thinking 'that's well and good for people I like – my friends, my family, even some of my colleagues – but some of the people I see in the office I can't stand! I just have to work alongside them.' Well, yes and no. Yes, because you're human and some people we find harder to like than others. And no, because you will be less effective if you can't find a way to like all your colleagues.

I bet you know who doesn't like you, even if they're not actually horrible to your face. They are the people who do the exact opposite of the list above. Think about it – the people you don't get on with:

- don't trust you;
- don't tell you the truth (and certainly not constructively);
- don't seek out and appear to enjoy your company;
- hold grudges against you;
- don't apologise and don't accept your apologies;
- don't understand you make mistakes and will blame you;
- if asked to help you out of a tight spot, do so grudgingly;
- don't let you know what's going on;

- don't offer to help you and most certainly would never ask you for help;
- wouldn't joke with you if it was their dying breath and being nice to you meant a heaven-ward trip rather than one in the other direction!

Aren't there people you don't like whom, if you think long and hard and honestly about it, you treat in the same way as described above? Even if subconsciously?

Above all, we're human beings, with our foibles, fallibilities and failings, and it is incredibly difficult to build a strong relationship with someone you don't like. It's frequently said that you don't have to like someone – you just have to respect them. But honestly, I can't think of many people I really dislike whom I also respect (although, in fairness, I pretty much like most people).

What I'm saying is: don't settle for just tolerating someone. Looking to find something to like in other folk is a useful skill. You don't have to want to be best mates with someone but it really helps if you find it relatively easy to be in their company. You can almost always find something to like about them if you try hard enough.

He's creating good relationships

This isn't just about making you a nicer person, of course! The point is that no matter how skilled you think you are in disguising your true feelings about someone, generally, people will know how much you like them by how you behave towards them.

You might say that deliberately changing your feelings about someone is very difficult to achieve, but it's probably easier than you think. I have a model I use to help change the way I view others and how they view me. I call it the Worm Cycle.

The Worm Cycle

All of us have belief sets. These sets range from fundamental beliefs about life to more ephemeral beliefs about situations and people. Almost all of our behaviour is influenced by those beliefs. If we believe negative things about ourselves or others, our behaviour will subconsciously reflect those beliefs, which will reinforce them. This cycle will continue, and we will be trapped in a belief set and way of behaving which may be unhelpful to us.

This diagram illustrates what I mean.

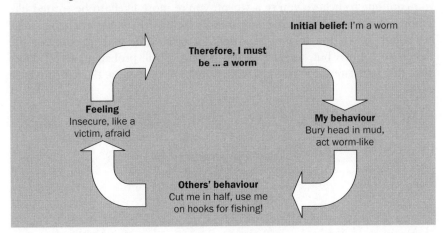

It is quite difficult to change our belief sets at the level of the beliefs themselves. Years of therapy can't even always do that. But we don't have to let our beliefs drive our behaviour if the behaviour is not working for us. We can break the cycle by ignoring or parking our beliefs and behaving in a way that reflects a different belief.

For example, it is extremely difficult to get others to treat you differently if you are behaving like a worm. It is also very difficult to change your belief set simply by deciding to. However, it is relatively easy to change your own behaviour because, although you don't really have conscious control over your beliefs, you do have control over your behaviour. So this is the most effective place to start. What you have to do is mirror the behaviour of a different belief set – if you want to be treated like a lion, you behave like a lion.

The Worm Cycle: becoming a lion!

So, you believe you're a worm, but you want to be a lion. The simplest way to achieve this is to change your behaviour to what lions do.

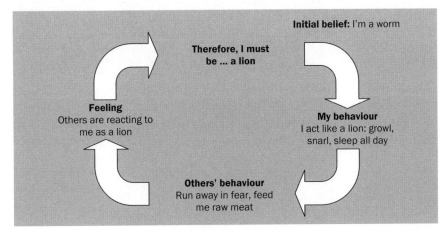

Eventually, you may well begin to believe that you are a lion. But, even if you continue to believe you're a worm, you're more likely to be treated like a lion. This change in behaviour doesn't result in people changing their behaviour in relation to you overnight. It takes time and practice for the change to happen but, as long as you persist, it will probably pay off. How does this translate into working with people? Well, here is the Worm Cycle again:

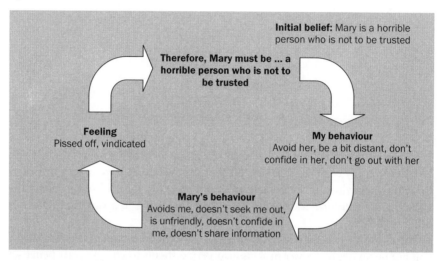

And here's how you might use the Worm Cycle to change your behaviour towards Mary:

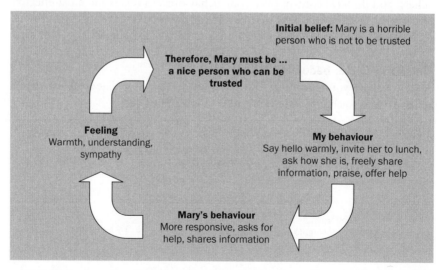

The point about this is that the change clearly isn't guaranteed, and Mary may indeed be a genuinely unpleasant person – although that is unlikely. What's more likely is that you are both reinforcing your beliefs by behaving in ways that demonstrate, no matter how subtly, your dislike of each other. But here's what I can guarantee: you stand a way better chance of building a healthier relationship with Mary if you start treating her more warmly and sympathetically.

What do people want?

One thing that pretty much every single human being on the planet has in common is the desire to be understood by others – and to be understood sympathetically. People want you to see them from their perspective, not from yours. A friend of mine says that 'people judge themselves by their motives and others by their actions'. What that means is that we ascribe good motives to ourselves when we do things, even if those things go wrong or cause harm or hurt to others. But we judge others by the behaviours we observe and tend to assume that others' motives aren't good. Trust me, pretty much everyone thinks they are a good, decent person who is misunderstood by others! Even in instances when we are being a bit mean or spiteful, we rarely admit it to ourselves, let alone to others. We rationalise our behaviour afterwards by saying that we were 'driven to it', that the person 'got what they deserved' and so on.

If you can convince people that you understand them, then you are going a long way towards creating really powerful relationships. And the only way to get to understand someone properly is to listen to them fully – listen to what they say, but also listen to what they do (i.e. observe their body language and facial expressions) and how they say the things they say (i.e. the volume and tone of their voice).

Listening

It's a funny thing. We are taught how to read, how to write and how to speak. But we're not taught how to listen. Somehow, it's assumed that it will just come naturally. Listening, however, is a skill you have to learn and work at. A basic ability to hear something is not the same as being able to truly listen. That being said, it can be amusing when someone accuses you of not listening when in fact you *were* listening (and understood the person fully) – you just didn't agree with what the person said!

The reason so many of us find it hard to properly listen is that we have so much stuff going on in our heads. Part of what has helped us as a species to survive and thrive is that we are constantly evaluating what's going on around us – what we are seeing, our physical sensations, the general environment around us and what we are hearing – so that we can make good choices about our actions. We rarely experience anything in a vacuum – it is always in the context of working out whether we are safe or under threat. And all of this happens at the deepest, most subconscious levels. Don't believe me? Well, have you ever been listening to someone and something they say diverts your mind into a whole different stream of thinking, and then suddenly you come to yourself to realise you'd stopped listening? Thought so! This is just an example of our brains assessing everything all the time.

I call this complex evaluation of everything that surrounds us listening with the six Es: our **ears**, our **eyes**, our **emotions**, our **experiences**, our **expectations** and our **egos**. I've put these six elements into a table with my thoughts about how to make sure we are minimising the distractions and maximising how we listen.

	What's happening	*What we can do*
Ears	Obviously we listen with our ears, but we listen for so much more than the words being used. The tone of voice, the pitch, the volume – all of these things will be influencing how we listen. For example, if we find the timbre of someone's voice irritating, it will affect our ability to take on board what they are saying. Other distractions (such as music, general white noise, roadworks and so on) can also make it hard to listen.	■ Focus on the words and their meaning. ■ Ask for clarification. ■ Summarise what you think the person said – check you've understood it. ■ For key conversations, such as one-to-ones, make sure that the environment is conducive to listening by minimising distractions.
Eyes	Using our eyes to help us to 'listen' is useful because people communicate through non-verbal means as well as their words. In fact, depending on the situation, up to 55% of face-to-face communication can be delivered through body language and facial expressions. Believe it or not, it really helps your listening if you look at people as they're talking.	■ Pay attention to body language – don't just listen to the words. For example, 'I'm fine' accompanied by a downbeat expression probably means the person isn't fine and you need to do something.

Emotions	There are two aspects to emotions: our emotional state when someone begins to talk to us, and our emotional reaction to what they say. Both of these things can get in the way of our ability to really hear what the other person is saying.	If you are in a bad mood when you need to talk to somebody, consider the following: ■ If you are able to, then ask the person to come back when you know you will be in a better frame of mind. ■ Use humour: tell the person you're a bit crabby and ask if they want to risk having a conversation with you. It'll put you in a better mood and help them to decide whether this is a good time. ■ Remind yourself that what the person needs to tell you is probably more important than how you are feeling, and get over yourself. ■ When you feel an emotional reaction to something someone has said, whether positive or negative, notice it and recognise that it might affect how well you are listening, then try to park it.
Experiences and expectations	Experiences and expectations are very closely linked. Our previous experience of people and situations will influence our expectations about what a person is really saying and what their 'hidden agenda' is, and that will affect our ability to listen. For example, if our experience of an individual is that they have a tendency to exaggerate, our expectation will be that they are going to exaggerate this time too, so we will hear them with this perception clouding our listening.	■ Remember that we genuinely don't know what is going on in other people's heads. ■ It's important to take each communication as a fresh one, without applying our previous experience with that person to what they are saying now.

Egos	Your ego is essentially your sense of self – or rather what you want to believe about yourself. Egos are not in and of themselves bad things, but they can sometimes get in the way of our listening if what the other person is saying feels damaging to our ego.	■ A healthy sense of self and a sense of humour help here. Recognising that pretty much most of the time what people are saying isn't actually directed at you or isn't a personal criticism will help you to listen more effectively.

Admittedly, all of the above is so much easier said than done. I've come to realise, though, that if I find a way to make myself really interested in what someone is saying, it's much easier to really listen to them.

Ask yourself, are you listening:

- to be right or to understand?
- for others' mistakes or for others' strengths?
- to prove you know best or to learn from another person?
- to make your point or to understand others' points?
- for what's possible or for what can't be done?
- as a know-it-all or as someone who wants to find out something new?
- for what you can do to help or to hear how the person has failed?

Working with your boss

I can polish this topic off in only a couple of paragraphs! Working with your boss is really not that hard. All you have to do is behave towards your boss the way you would like your team to behave towards you.

It's interesting how we allow people's job titles or positions to completely influence our view of them, regardless of any evidence of what the person is actually like. For example, if we learn that we're going to meet an MP, as soon as we hear those two letters we're full of opinions about what MPs are like. We then tend to assume the MP we are going to meet or talk to is going to be like our stereotypical view (even though MPs are individual human beings just as we are and are highly unlikely to all be the same). We know it's daft, but we all do it. But, at the very least, don't do it with your boss. Your boss is a human being who has the same hang-ups, fears and worries that you do. And, in the same way that you probably don't show your anxieties to your team members, so too your boss will almost certainly be hiding theirs.

Here is a simple list of what to do to get on with your boss:

- Be positive.
- Be a can-do person.
- Tell your boss when they do something that really helps you or the team.
- Be natural and yourself in their company.
- Assume that your boss is a nice human being who has the same struggles as you do and treat them accordingly.
- Ask their advice and listen to it.

- Offer your boss help and support when it seems like they need it.
- Include them in social invitations – but don't be offended if they say no.
- Keep your boss informed about what's going on in your team.
- Give your boss credit – they're probably doing their best (much as you are).

Don't lose sight of the fact that you are both working towards the same goal – delivering for your beneficiaries. You're on the same side.

Remember

1. You're not part of your team – you're the manager of it, so you need to manage your relationships appropriately.
2. Work hard at listening.
3. Treat your boss like a fellow human being.

10 Learning from others

Give every man thy ear but few thy voice:
Take each man's censure but reserve thy
judgment.
William Shakespeare, *Hamlet*, Act I, Scene III,
Polonius speaking to Laertes

Tips from fellow managers

The big thing to remember about your management experience is that you are not alone and pretty much nothing you will ever face has not at some point been faced by someone else. I find it's always useful and, indeed, reassuring to listen to the wisdom of those who have been where I am and have learned from it.

This chapter offers exactly that. It consists of key tips from managers of various levels of experience on what they have learned during their time as managers. I hope you find it as inspiring as I do.

Stuart Cole, Research Manager

- You can't do it all yourself, so trust and support those you manage to take ownership of key objectives. They'll become more capable and independent, allowing you to manage their tasks, not their work.
- Managers don't need to have all the answers, but we should know how to find solutions, so don't be afraid to ask people 'What do you recommend?' Discussing solutions with those you manage is a great way to teach your team to solve problems and also to learn from them.
- Take back control of your time by using your Outlook calendar. Add deadlines as you get them, plan your week ahead and follow your plan for the day. This way you can concentrate on your work rather than on your workload.
- Go paperless, if you can. A small computer is the best way to have everything at your fingertips and keep yourself organised wherever you are.
- Plan for succession. Those you manage should be able to do your job as well as you can, so train them and trust them to step up when the time comes.

Bronwen Edwards, Executive Office Manager

- You don't have to know everything – it's okay to have to go and find the answer.

- Having to ask your senior manager for advice, help or direction does not mean you're failing (it helps to stroke their ego too!).
- It takes some time to accept this one, but don't take everything to heart – a disagreement over a policy or a decision is not an attack on you personally.
- Make sure you save those nice and positive emails to look through when you're having a bad day.
- Say 'yes' to doing the scary things: go to the event at the House of Commons because you've never been before; offer to lead the staff away day; accept the public-speaking invite; and convince your team members to do the same!

Jay Kennedy, Director of Policy and Research
- Your staff members are human beings. But we sometimes pretend that people are robots that can be slotted into work plans and organograms. In fact, they're complex emotional creatures – just like you – with a world of passions, talents, motivations, fears and worries outside their day job. Take an interest in those things that are important to your staff.
- It's always hard to get the right balance between giving people sufficient structure to achieve against expectations and giving them enough freedom to innovate and own their work. The balance is constantly shifting and rarely settles. It's different for different people in different circumstances. If you sense this and are thinking about it all the time, you're doing it right.
- Trust your instincts, but be wary of how your own personal issues might be affecting your judgement. Just because you're inexperienced doesn't mean you're wrong or your approach isn't the right one. Find peers you can trust, and test your thinking with them in confidence.
- Always do your level best to remain calm and focused on solutions, especially in crisis situations when others are freaking out or demonstrating challenging behaviour.
- If you're putting lots of thinking and effort into recruiting the right people, or promoting them to new roles, that's a good thing. This also holds for making tough decisions about discipline or letting people go. These big decisions will be the making of you. But, even if you get it wrong, that's OK – you just have to deal with it and learn for the next time. Mistakes are human and always easier to see in hindsight because we cannot predict the future!

George Knight, Head of Sales and Customer Services
- Always have, what I call, a causal approach when dealing with your team. You have to act, even if it may seem easier not to interfere, if you want your team to know that actions have repercussions. For example, if you don't deal with issues such as lateness in a timely manner, the problem can spiral as other individuals on your team may take that as a sign it is OK to be late.

- Remember: it is OK for your team to fail. In fact, it is essential that you create an environment where it is safe for your team members to fail and learn from their mistakes. Even if you know the answer to a query, by letting your team members unearth their own solution you will make them own that solution.
- You are not the manager of a team because you are an expert on each of your team members' jobs. In fact, it is the opposite: they should all be the experts on what they do and your role as the manager should simply be to support them to perform those tasks to the best of their ability.
- As a manager, you have to make time for your team. Don't bite off more than you can chew, and be realistic about any projects you would like to run. It is far more effective to tackle small, bite-sized chunks of work one at a time than to take on a massive project that could cause you to neglect your team.
- Use your diary. It is unfair to spring any surprise one-to-ones or meetings on your team. Every regular meeting should be scheduled in your team members' calendars as a recurring event so that neither you nor they miss it.

Annette Lewis, Development Manager

- Have a mentor – someone who has been or currently is a manager that you can go to for guidance and support.
- Communicate openly and honestly – the good, the bad and the ugly.
- Don't act like you know everything; you do not and are not expected to.
- Your new role will have new responsibilities and expectations, but your core values will always remain the same no matter what your position is; know these and stand by them at all times. These values will help to guide you during difficult times, regardless of your role or situation.
- Read, watch, train, talk … Always strive to develop yourself, your role and your knowledge in any way you can.

Denise Lillya, Research Manager

- Encourage people to be generous with their knowledge, skills and ideas, and not to be precious about their work; it is our shared knowledge and development that helps improve the organisation.
- Know your team members' strengths and weaknesses, and know their backgrounds – maybe they even had a life before joining your organisation! Develop their strengths and encourage them to address their 'weaknesses' with training and confidence-building.
- Don't set yourself apart; managers have a different role but are not a different species.
- Kill gossip. One of the fastest ways to destroy team spirit and good morale is to allow discontent to spread. If there's a problem, it's your job to sort it out and bring the team back together.

- Don't procrastinate. Seek good advice but deal with issues as they arise, particularly the difficult ones. Don't allow problems to fester – they can become contagious.

John Martin, Publisher

- Don't immediately assume a new 'managerial' personality with your new team as it will seem fake – this will evolve over time.
- Invest early in connecting with other managers and understanding what they need from you as a colleague.
- Get to know the team you are managing and their strengths and weaknesses.
- As you are new, initially your main strength will be the potential of bringing fresh ideas and a new perspective to the management team. In the early weeks, write down what doesn't seem to make sense about the job on a piece of paper and tuck it away in a drawer. Later, pull it out and see what still doesn't add up, and then find out more or make suggestions for changes.
- Start prepared. Find out as much as you can about your new organisation and/or job – the vision and mission, the latest accounts and what other departments do.

Justin Martin, Marketing Manager

- Whatever your own workload is, you always need to create time and space to support your team members on a regular basis (don't move this time with them or de-prioritise it).
- Start one-to-ones by asking how the person is and take an interest in their life outside work. Seems obvious, but it's always good to know how they are doing in their personal life, if they have any problems and so on.
- Connect what your team does to the organisation's vision and mission as much as possible and as frequently as possible. This will help to keep motivation high in the team and individual roles.
- Support, and get support from, your fellow managers. They've been or are going through the same journey you are now on – you will be able to help each other along the way.
- When recruiting, remember that how you think the person will fit into the organisation (i.e. how much they understand why the organisation exists and so on) is just as important as how qualified they are for the role.

Chibuzo Okpala, Finance Director

- Take off the technical specialist hat and put on the management hat. Becoming a good manager is not about being an expert in your technical field. It is more about seeing the way in which your team can build relationships with other teams and help other teams do better.

- You do not have to know it all. It's OK not to know everything about your area of responsibility. What you have to do is to know your critical success and failure points very well; have general knowledge on regularly practised areas of responsibility (enough to discuss and learn more if needed); and ensure you have access to skills and knowledge on the rarely practised areas of responsibility.
- Your staff members are your best asset (not you). Your ability to get the work done is not down to your brilliance in preparing reports and things like that; it is down to your ability to get your staff to do what you need them to do to get the reports, analysis, functions and so on ready.
- Connect to your peers – they often see things you don't see. Your fellow managers are likely to have multiple skills and will know a bit about other areas of responsibility outside their own. While they may not know half of what you know about your speciality, they have the benefit of seeing your areas without the blinkers of your particular responsibility and, therefore, will be able to think outside your 'box'.
- Ensure that your work is fit for purpose. Your success as a manager is not just about doing your listed job tasks; it is about making sure that your output is what is needed by the role at that moment to support the organisation. Ensure that you have some regular time to sit down to reflect: time to put away the list of tasks which outline your role and think of what is needed from you. This way, you can be proactive regarding the needs of the organisation, ensure that you are responding to the changing operating environment, and hence gain the trust of your boss and colleagues by showing that you know what you are doing.

Tom Traynor, Head of Research
- Use your knowledge and experience to enable you to ask the right questions to find the best solutions to move forward.
- Show empathy and listen to other people's points of view.
- Try to be consistent – giving out mixed messages about your expectations creates uncertainty, which is counterproductive.
- Build a strong team and look for skills and experience that fill gaps in knowledge. Don't be afraid to learn from others.
- Delegate responsibilities among your team and trust them to get on with the job. This is empowering and usually brings out the best in people, but ensure they have your support when needed.

John Wallace, Director of Operations
- Praise, praise and praise some more. Ignore any 'I don't like compliments' or, as I have witnessed, a physical wince when you give praise to someone. In my opinion, we can never hear compliments enough and, whether we consciously admit it or not, a well-thought-out recognition of performance is worth way more than any pay rise. Just look people in the eye and mean it.

- Notice when performance has slipped and deal with it straight away. If you start to find that someone you manage isn't doing what you asked of them, act. Don't just whinge and moan about it.
- Repeatedly reminding someone to do something you asked of them can be infuriating. But that's part of your job and reminding generally works. I keep in mind the following: we do what we like doing and what our boss checks up on. Everything else goes on a list!
- Always start with purpose. When discussing any project, whether in a formal meeting or an informal conversation, always keep the reason for the project in the forefront of your mind. If the meeting or conversation starts to descend into reasons why the project is too difficult or there isn't enough time, or something similar, then bring it back to the purpose. Whatever the problem is, the project is possible and there will be time for it, if it is really needed.
- If you're not fighting back, then you're probably not doing your job. It's so easy to just go along with what your team wants. As a manager, you will have access to information that those you manage won't have, so often what they believe is the right way forward won't be the right way at all, simply because they don't know the full story. So, if your default response is to smile and nod, work at listening and answering with questions such as 'How would that work?' or 'Have you thought about how that might affect … ?'

Remember

1. You're not alone – someone's been there, done that and got the T-shirt.
2. Don't be afraid to ask for help and advice.
3. Try new things.

References and notes

Page x – **Introduction epigraph:** Paraphrased variation of 'If our foresight were as good as our hindsight, we'd be better off by a damn sight': Doyle Charles, Mieder Wolfgang and Shapiro Fred (eds), *The Dictionary of Modern Proverbs*, New Haven, Yale University Press, 2012, p. 121.

Page 1 – **Chapter 1 epigraph:** This quote is widely attributed to Peter F. Drucker, US management consultant, although its origin is unconfirmed.

Page 2 – **Debra Allcock Tyler's book:** Debra Allcock Tyler, *It's Tough at the Top*, London, Directory of Social Change, 2017.

Page 11 – **Chapter 2 epigraph:** Lewis Carroll, *Alice's Adventures in Wonderland*, New York, Harper and Brothers, 1901, p. 179.

Page 25 – **Chapter 3 epigraph:** This quote has been attributed to Eleanor Roosevelt, American politician, diplomat and activist, although its origin is unconfirmed.

Page 27 – **Action-centred leadership:** See John Adair, *Action-Centred Leadership*, London, McGraw-Hill, 1973.

Page 30 – **A simple toolbox:** The table is adapted from Edwin Smith and Colin Chase, *The Manager as a Leader (Notes for Managers)*, London, Industrial Society Press, 1989.

Page 30 – **Liberating leadership:** See David Turner, *Liberating Leadership*, London, Industrial Society Press, 1998.

Page 31 – **Outstanding leadership:** Penny Tamkin, Gemma Pearson, Wendy Hirsh and Susannah Constable, *Exceeding Expectations: The principles of outstanding leadership*, London, The Work Foundation, 2010.

Page 32 – **Differences between good and outstanding leaders table:** Penny Tamkin, Gemma Pearson, Wendy Hirsh and Susannah Constable, *Exceeding Expectations: The principles of outstanding leadership – Executive summary*, London, The Work Foundation, 2010, p. 5.

Page 33 – **Characteristics of outstanding leaders table:** Penny Tamkin, Gemma Pearson, Wendy Hirsh and Susannah Constable, *Exceeding Expectations: The principles of outstanding leadership*, London, The Work Foundation, 2010, pp. 89–91.

Page 41 – **Chapter 4 epigraph:** This quote is attributed to Johann Wolfgang von Goethe, although its origin is unconfirmed.

Page 43 – **Jane Austen's quote:** Jane Austen, *Pride and Prejudice*, Oxford, Oxford University Press, 1984, p. 60.

Page 44 – **Maslow's hierarchy of needs:** Abraham Maslow, 'A Theory of Human Motivation', *Psychological Review*, vol. 50, 1943, pp. 370–96.

Page 47 – **Research on money as motivator:** For a meta-analysis of the research on this topic, see Timothy A. Judge, Ronald F. Piccolo, Nathan P. Podsakoff, John C. Shaw and Bruce L. Rich, 'The Relationship between Pay and Job Satisfaction: A meta-analysis of the literature', *Journal of Vocational Behavior*, vol. 77, no. 2, pp. 157–67.

Page 48 – **McGregor's Theory X and Theory Y:** Douglas McGregor, *The Human Side of Enterprise*, New York, McGraw-Hill, 1960.

Page 59 – **Chapter 5 epigraph:** If you happen to know where this quote originates, do get in touch!

Page 63 – **Muzafer Sherif's experiment:** Muzafer Sherif, *The Psychology of Social Norms*, New York, Harper and Brothers, 1936.

Page 64 – **Solomon Asch's experiment:** Solomon Asch, 'Effects of Group Pressure upon the Modification and Distortion of Judgments', in *Groups, Leadership and Men: Research in human relations*, edited by H. Guetzkow, Oxford, Carnegie Press, 1951, pp. 177–90.

Page 64 – **Diagrams used in Solomon Asch's experiment:** Fred the Oyster, 'Asch experiment', https://commons.wikimedia.org/wiki/File:Asch_experiment.svg, 2014, accessed 18 August 2018.

Page 65 – **Margaret Wetherell's experiments:** Margaret Wetherell, 'Social Identity and Group Polarization' in J. C. Turner et al., *Rediscovering the Social Group: a self-categorization theory*, Oxford, Blackwell, 1987, pp. 142–70.

Page 66 – **Kurt Lewin's experiment:** Kurt Lewin, 'Forces behind Food Habits and Methods of Change', in *The Problem of Changing Food Habits: Report of the Committee on Food*, Washington, DC, National Academy of Sciences, National Research Council, 1943, pp. 35–65.

Page 68 – **Bruce Tuckman's stages of group development:** Bruce Tuckman, 'Developmental Sequence in Small Groups', *Psychological Bulletin*, vol. 63, no. 6, 1965, pp. 384–99.

Page 71 – **Chapter 6 epigraph:** Henry Wadsworth Longfellow, 'The Village Blacksmith', in *Ballads and Other Poems*, Cambridge, MA, John Owen, 1842, p. 101.

Page 72 – **Quote on planning:** These words have been attributed to Sun Tzu, although the origin of the quote is unconfirmed.

Page 78 – **Quote on the benefits of delegation:** Margaret Lloyd and Brian Rothwell, *Leadership 101*, London, Directory of Social Change, 2007, p. 225.

Page 82 – **Your plan vs reality diagram:** Philippe Martin, 'Plan vs Reality', www.flickr.com/photos/lafabriquedeblogs/10927616053, 2013, accessed 3 September 2018.

Page 83 – **Chapter 7 epigraph:** A paraphrased variation of 'It is not that we have a short space of time, but that we waste much of it. ... So it is – the life we receive is not short, but we make it so, nor do we have any lack of it, but are wasteful of it.' in Lucius Annaeus Seneca, *On the Shortness of Life*, translated by John W. Basore, Loeb Classical Library [web page], www.forumromanum.org/literature/index.html, accessed 20 October 2018.

Page 84 – **Average amount of hours a night people in the UK sleep:** *The Great British Bedtime Report* [PDF], www.sleepcouncil.org.uk/wp-content/uploads/2013/02/The-Great-British-Bedtime-Report.pdf, 2013, p. 30, accessed 31 August 2018.

Page 85 – **Survey of office workers on common distractions:** 'New CareerBuilder survey reveals how much smartphones are sapping productivity at work' [web page], www.careerbuilder.co.uk, 2016, accessed 3 September 2018.

Page 97 – **Chapter 8 epigraph:** Caron Bradshaw in an email to the author, January 2018.

Page 107 – **Chapter 9 epigraph:** This quote is widely attributed to Theodore Roosevelt, US president, although its origin is unconfirmed.

Page 114 – **The amount of communication delivered through body language and facial expressions:** According to the research undertaken in the 1970s by Albert Mehrabian (see Albert Mehrabian and Susan Ferris, 'Inference of attitudes from nonverbal communication in two channels', *Journal of Consulting Psychology*, Vol. 31(3), 1967, pp. 248–52; and Albert Mehrabian and Morton Wiener, 'Decoding of inconsistent communications', *Journal of Personality and Social Psychology*, Vol. 6(1), 1967, pp. 109–14), face-to-face communication consist of 55% body language and facial expressions, 38% voice tone and 7% actual words used. Note, however, that Mehrabian has clarified that such findings apply when communication is about feelings or attitudes, not in other cases (see Albert Mehrabian, *Silent messages: Implicit communication of emotions and attitudes*, Wadsworth, 1981).

Page 119 – **Chapter 10 epigraph:** William Shakespeare, *Hamlet, Prince of Denmark*, Act I, Scene III.

Recommended reading

Allcock Tyler, Debra, *It's Tough at the Top*, 2017, Directory of Social Change

Allcock Tyler, Debra, *The Pleasure and the Pain*, 2007, Directory of Social Change

Carnegie, Dale, *How to Win Friends and Influence People*, 1998, Pocket Books

Dalton, Dorothy, *Financial Governance*, 2017, Rathbones and ACEVO – a handy review of the basics in charity accounting

Goleman, Daniel, *Emotional Intelligence: Why it can matter more than IQ*, 2005, Bantam Books

Greenfield, Susan, *The Private Life of the Brain*, 2000, Allen Lane (The Penguin Press)

Hackman, Richard, *Leading Teams: Setting the stage for great performances*, 2002, Harvard Business School Press

Harris, Thomas, *I'm OK – You're OK*, 1996, Avon Books

Hudson, Mike, *Managing Without Profit*, 2017, Directory of Social Change

Johnson, Dr Spencer, *Who Moved my Cheese?*, 2002, Vermillion

Kahneman, Daniel, *Thinking, Fast and Slow*, 2012, Penguin

Lawson, Ian, *Leaders for Tomorrow's Society*, 1999, Industrial Society Press

McCurley, Steve, Lynch, Rick and Jackson, Rob, *The Complete Volunteer Management Handbook*, 2012, Directory of Social Change

Maslow, Abraham, *The Hierarchy of Needs*, 1999, Chartered Management Institute

Milne, A. A. and Shepherd, E. H., *Winnie the Pooh's Little Book of Wisdom*, 1999, Methuen

Morgan, Gareth, *The Charity Treasurer's Handbook*, 2017, Directory of Social Change – for those of you in need of some more in-depth knowledge of your charity's finance

Olivier, Richard, *Inspirational Leadership: Henry V and the Muse of Fire – Timeless insights from Shakespeare's greatest* leader, 2003, Spiro Press

Pinker, Stephen, *How the Mind works*, 2009, W.W. Norton and Company

Rosling, Hans, *Factfulness*, 2018, Sceptre

Rothwell, Brian, *Team Building*, 2009, Directory of Social Change

Rowntree, Derek, *The Manager's Book of Checklists*, 2006, Pearson Education Ltd

Wright, Chrissie, *Motivating Staff*, 2010, Directory of Social Change

Zeldin, Theodore, *Conversation: How talk can change your life*, 1998, Harvill Press

Index